CW01020913

ROYAL ENFIELD

A COMPLETE HISTORY

1964

Royal Enfield

TT 250

Geoff Duke O.B.E. (FIVE TIMES WORLD CHAMPION) rides Royal Enfield

ROYAL ENFIELD

A COMPLETE HISTORY

THE CROWOOD PRESS

First published in 2021 by
The Crowood Press Ltd
Ramsbury, Marlborough
Wiltshire SN8 2HR

enquiries@crowood.com

www.crowood.com

British Library Cataloguing-in-Publication Data
A catalogue record for this book is available from the British Library.

ISBN 978 1 78500 852 8

Typeset by Simon and Sons
Cover design by Maggie Mellett

Printed and bound in India by Parksons Graphics Pvt. Ltd., Mumbai.

CONTENTS

INTRODUCTION

My interest in Royal Enfield started with a very particular, and really quite peculiar, event: the appearance in our local motorcycle dealer's shop window of an old Interceptor parallel twin. Richard Stevens' eponymous business is a long-standing Yamaha dealership, a follow-on from a fine road-racing career. I had first admired Richard as a front runner in the North Gloucestershire Motor Cycle Club races, which cheerfully ignored the fact that our local circuits – Castle Combe, Keevil, Wroughton, Hullavington and Colerne – were far south of Gloucester, in deepest Wiltshire. Only Castle Combe survives as a race track today, although Wroughton was included in *The Grand Tour* – the Amazon show featuring Jeremy Clarkson, James May and Richard Hammond – as a test track, the Eboladrome (apparently when viewed from above its layout bears a similarity to the profile of the Ebola virus).

But back in the 1970s and well into the 1980s, these circuits – old RAF bases, with perimeter tracks pressed into road-racing service – regularly hosted full programmes of motorcycle racing, cheered on by thousands of local fans. Car parks heaved with everything from sports mopeds, through the last of the big British bikes, to the latest Japanese rocket ships. The car parks were almost worth the price of admission alone as a giant motorcycle show, while the racers in the pits found themselves on the end of countless fans' questions and good wishes of Godspeed. And one of those racers was Richard Stevens, a quietly spoken local mechanic with a fierce turn of pace that had won him the Avon Tyres' 250 national production title – sponsored by *Bike* magazine – in 1975. Richard had previously competed in the Ultra Lightweight TT that claimed Gilberto Parlotti's life in 1972 and heralded the end of the road for the Isle of Man's hosting of the British motorcycle Grand Prix. His final TT entry was in the 1978 Formula 3 race on a Honda Yoshimura 460 four that I had sold to his sponsor after a crash. This was the year of Mike Hailwood's famous return to the Island.

OPPOSITE: **The new Interceptor in chrome at the Royal Enfield Café and mini-museum in Goa.**

So when Richard stuck a restored Royal Enfield Interceptor – an archetypal big British vertical twin from the feted post-war boom – in his Devizes shop window in 2009, I had to ask why. This is a small-scale, old-school dealership with a bell on the front door that inevitably summons Richard from the workshop in the hope of selling some off-road spares or a new 12V battery. Or, on this occasion, a nosy neighbour wanting to ask about the old fogey in the window. What I discovered over the next few minutes became a cover story for the bestselling *Classic Bike* magazine in 2010, with editor Ben Miller cheerfully caning the Interceptor along the Devizes to Swindon road. It turned out that Richard wasn't so much quietly spoken as completely silent on his part in a hugely important part of British motorcycling history, of which he had been a first-hand witness.

Richard casually told me that he had been the development rider for Royal Enfield's Interceptor, based at the Bradford-on-Avon workshop, which was actually an old mine that

Chrome and Candy Crush Orange Interceptors on the beach. ROYAL ENFIELD

the Redditch factory had adopted as a safe haven for World War II but somehow never left. The Wiltshire branch of Royal Enfield actually outlived the original Worcestershire facilities, not only expecting Richard to test the bike's reliability by piling on the road miles, but also proving its speed at MIRA (the Motor Industry Research Association) in Warwickshire – and now the home of Royal Enfield's research and development base, which recently invited Richard to sample the Interceptor's modern namesake. When Enfield folded in the UK Richard was working on an 800 Interceptor that he wound up to 128mph (206km/h) at MIRA, alongside (and overtaking) a dumbstruck Percy Tait testing a Trident. ('Percy Tait was like a farmer – well, he was a farmer.' Thank you, Richard, another childhood hero brought down to size.)

Richard raced and won on the Interceptor – *Motor Cycle News* (MCN) made much of this with a front-page splash showing 'Cal Rayborn trying out the new racer'. But it turns out that the photograph was taken riding round Heston Services car park, Richard having brought the bike up in a van, and he even had to lend the mighty Rayborn his riding kit. Inevitably nostalgia caught up with Richard, so he tracked down and restored the Interceptor before placing it in his window.

'You must have seen these in old magazines,' Richard queried, shuffling through a shelfful of memorabilia – topped by TT Replicas awarded for his Isle of Man races. No, I definitely had not seen the yellowing magazines, but then I didn't start buying motorcycle publications until 1975, when Richard was winning championships on his Yamaha RD250. Yet there he was, late sixties monochrome cool looking sideways into the camera in Geoff Duke style one-piece black leathers aboard one of the fastest British motorcycles of the era.

Richard Stevens (left) on Series 2 Interceptor racer c.1970 with Chris Ludgate on a Series 1. Note Richard's TT100 front tyre, the latest thing from Dunlop. RICHARD STEVENS

Richard Stevens with his restored Interceptor on a freezing February photoshoot for *Classic Bike* magazine.

'So,' I ventured, 'was that the best bike you ever rode?' Richard looked aghast. 'No, that would be the Suzuki Super Six. That was a lovely bike, especially on the Isle of Man.' My antennae were reset to business as usual and Richard's association with quarter-litre, two-stroke, six-speed twins was confirmed. British bikes really were so last century. Even today, Richard's as happy to parade a Japanese light-weight at Mallory Park's Festival of 1000 bikes as he is to show off the big Enfield.

And yet, my curiosity had been piqued and to discover such a gap in my knowledge of local history, never mind motorcycling knowledge, was a shock. So a few days later I parked my Ducati Monster close to the entrance of the old mine that had been the Royal Enfield factory entrance and from which Richard had fired an Interceptor on timeless occasions fifty years earlier. Greeted by a stocky chap with a ponytail and fluorescent vest, our initial rapport cooled when I asked if I might see what lay inside. Secure storage apparently. No chance of a visit. Hardly surprising, given that some of these mines were converted to a prospective home for the British government if World War III ever happened. At a dead end, I went home and rang the people at *Classic*

Bike magazine. Yes, they'd love Richard's story. So I wrote it, they printed it and I forgot about Royal Enfield.

But inevitably Richard's tales led to trails to follow and a visit to India made me appreciate that while a 350 Bullet single might be small beer in the UK, it was a fine claret with a personal sommelier in its adopted home. The pride the locals have for Royal Enfield is remarkable; two examples of this are, firstly, noticing an unloved Tata Nano – the super cheap microcar that UK business pages once declared the nemesis of motorcycling in India and a possible future hit in European cities – I asked a young local why they never became popular. 'They sound like a tuk-tuk,' he laughed. 'Anyway you could buy a 350 Bullet for the same money,' he added with a certainty that even an Englishman out in the midday sun could not argue with.

The second revelation came on the road to the Royal Enfield Café in northern Goa, when we were overtaken by a 350 Bullet. 'The best motorcycle in India,' offered the taxi driver. 'Never mind all the Japanese bikes. It's the *sound* of a Royal Enfield: it makes you happy.' His smile proved that this was true. My determination to delve into Royal Enfield's history, both in the UK and India, was settled.

A Bullet overtakes our taxi in Goa in January 2020: 'The sound of a Royal Enfield: it makes you happy,' offered the driver.

And then, in a bout of serendipity, a friend and fellow Ducati obsessive inherited his father's Model K, a mighty pre-war Royal Enfield V-twin: he liked it, and I was intrigued.

I seem to have come full circle, from sceptic to fan. My first impression of Royal Enfield came courtesy of a road test in December 1977's *Bike* magazine. At £695, the Indian-built 350 Bullet was pricier than a Japanese 250 twin, despite having such modest performance that the tester reported 'hills flattened its acceleration to less than that of a Honda 125 single' and the front brake was 'terrifyingly ineffective'. Back then, Norton-Villiers Triumph (NVT), the dying breath of the British motorcycle industry, owned a 30 per cent stake in Enfield's Indian outpost and had considered importing the Bullet before Slater Brothers – of Laverda Jota fame – stepped in. But that 1977 test under the headline 'At last, the 1952 show' concluded with NVT chairman Dennis Poore observing that 'following an evaluation of the 350 Bullet no one seemed that keen [on importing it]'. Famed journalist Peter Watson added 'I think I know why'.

Yet here we are more than forty years later with Enfield's star rising once more, their bargain basement pricing no indication of the massive leap in quality (and brakes!) that now outshines far more expensive marques. Many have come and gone, but Enfield has remained a constant, ignoring fashion in favour of an honest, straightforward motorcycling experience. Yet there has been glamour, innovation and competition success as well along the way. The Royal Enfield story includes a glorious past, a promising future and much to relish in achievement spanning three centuries. Royal Enfield's famous motto – 'made like a gun' – hints at the factory's origins, but few appreciate that it is the oldest motorcycle manufacturer boasting continuous production in existence. In addition, its famous Bullet can claim the longest motorcycle production run of all time. When the factory produced its first powered vehicles, the horse was still the fastest means of transport.

The origins of the Royal Enfield marque can be traced back to a small light engineering firm founded in Redditch, Worcestershire, in mid-Victorian times to make needles. Expanding into bicycle manufacture by the turn of the century, it morphed into the Enfield Cycle Company, makers of the 'Royal Enfield' bicycle. The first powered vehicles came in the twilight years of the nineteenth century with the first motorcycles around 1900. By 1904, the firm was concentrating on motor cars, resuming motorcycle manufacture in 1910 with a Swiss Motosacoche V-twin. The famous JAP V-twin sidecar outfit joined the range for 1912 and the firm continued the V-twin theme with a new solo for 1913, powered by Enfield's own engine, racing successfully at Brooklands and the Isle of Man TT. Enfield was by now recognized as a technically advanced factory, adopting multi-speed transmission, chain drive, automatic dry-sump lubrication and a patented cush-drive rear hub that would remain a feature of all future models and was supplied to other manufacturers.

The Ashleigh works, Redditch, on Bromsgrove Road, a short distance from and very similar to the original. It is an old needle-making factory with the owner's villa beside, looking very similar to the Givry works at Hunt End that were the beginnings of Royal Enfield. J. THOMAS

ROYAL ENFIELD

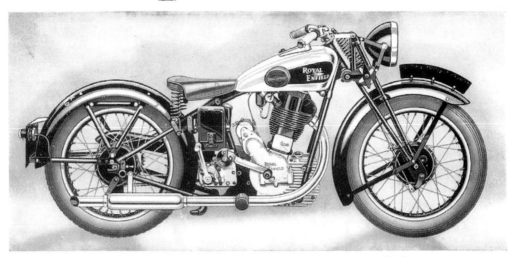

Terrific speed and acceleration combined with amazing road-holding qualities.

Abridged Specification (see page 5).

ENGINE - -	488 c.c. single cylinder. Bore and stroke 85·5 × 85 m/m. Tuned engine with high compression piston. Over-head valves, rocker gear and push rods totally enclosed and automatically lubricated.	
LUBRICATION	Royal Enfield dry-sump circulating system, oil container in crankcase.	
CARBURETTOR	Twist grip control to throttle, handle bar lever control to air slide.	
GEARBOX - -	Heavyweight four-speed with positive change foot control. Hand-controlled four-speed gear, if desired, without extra charge. Standard ratios : Solo, 5, 6·5, 9 and 13·9 to 1. Sidecar, 5·8, 7·6, 10·4, and 16·1 to 1.	

IGNITION AND LIGHTING SET	Lucas 6-volt Magdyno set, gear-driven from engine. Control panel in tank.
BRAKES - -	Internal expanding, front and rear, 6½in. diameter. Ribbed drums.
TRANSMISSION	Front chain totally enclosed in cast aluminium oil-bath case.
REAR WHEEL	The rear wheel on this model has a knock-out spindle. On withdrawal of this, a distance piece can be removed leaving a gap sufficient to enable an inner tube to be changed without removing the wheel.
TYRES - -	Dunlop cord, 26 × 3·25in.
STAND - -	Patented central prop stand.
FINISH - -	Best quality black enamel. Bright parts, including tank, wheel rims and handlebar, chromium plated.

Model LO "500 BULLET"
INCLUDING ELECTRIC LIGHTING SET

The 500 Bullet in the 1935 catalogue.

The GT 535 with Harris Performance (now part of Royal Enfield's UK base) frame and styling.

The legendary single-cylinder Bullet was born in 1932 and first displayed at the Olympia Motorcycle Show in London. Radical redesigns in 1936 and 1948 prepared the Bullet for export on a huge scale, with work starting in 1955 on a factory in India that allowed Royal Enfield to survive the collapse of the marque in the UK.

In 1941, Royal Enfield moved some production from Redditch to old underground stone workings in Wiltshire, an abandoned mine for the famous Bath stone. Safely hidden from Nazi bombers, sights for anti-aircraft guns and control equipment for Bofors guns were built, but at the end of the war somehow the factory failed to repatriate to Redditch. Instead, returning to motorcycles, the 248cc Crusader, Meteor and Meteor Minor were built at Bradford-on-Avon until 1963. The Interceptor and Constellation 692 and 736cc twins were also built there until 1970, outliving the Redditch factory's closure in 1967.

And there Royal Enfield would have ended, another nail in the coffin of the British motorcycle industry. But, pleased with their Enfield singles, the Indian Army and government literally bit the bullet and bought what was left of the business. The legend lived on, initially as cheap and cheerful (or not) reminders of how motorcycles used to be, albeit often falling behind Western expectations of quality and reliability.

But in recent years new owners have taken Royal Enfield back to quality and its roots, with a wave of new models including the big twin-cylinder Interceptor and the Continental GT. And, just as importantly, a UK research and development facility has been established – Royal Enfield is coming home.

So this story of Royal Enfield has a lot of ground to cover, from details of the most important models down the years from both UK factories, together with the lifeline and future that is the Indian connection. The experience of owners both in the UK and India will contrast the demands of both markets and the ambition of the new factory that has even hinted at reviving the layout that Royal Enfield was originally famous for – a mighty V-twin. With a history that spans three centuries there's a lot to pack in.

But first, some thanks. To Richard Stevens, obviously, and as always to Pat Slinn, late of BSA for answering questions. Steve Smith of Avon tyres was a great help, as was Ivar de Gier, famous for his photography collection under the A Herl Inc. banner. And I am especially indebted to Bonhams for photographs, especially James Stensel. With many staff furloughed, James spent an age finding and sending me high-resolution images simply as an act of goodwill. It's a privilege to work alongside him and the rest of the Bonhams motorcycle team.

TIMELINE

1851 Redditch chosen by George Townsend to set up a business making sewing needles.

1882 Townsend's son, also George, added bicycle component manufacturing to the company's product range, including saddles and forks.

1886 Complete bicycles being sold under the Townsend and Ecossais banner.

1891 Townsend suffers financial collapse and by November his bankers settle on Albert Eadie and Bob Walker Smith to take over the business.

1892 Townsend is reborn as the Eadie Manufacturing Company Limited.

1893 Eadie wins a contract to supply precision parts to the Royal Small Arms Factory of Enfield, Middlesex. To celebrate, the company rechristens its undertaking the Enfield Manufacturing Company and launches its first bicycle as the Enfield.

1898 Enfield launches a motorized vehicle known as a Quadricycle built around two robust bicycle frames and powered by a proprietary 1½HP De Dion engine.

1901 The first Royal Enfield motorcycle built.

1907 Eadie Manufacturing, the cycling and firearms business, sold to BSA.

1909 Royal Enfield's first V-twin, using a Motosacoche engine shown at the Stanley Cycle Show.

1912 First JAP V-twin powered Royal Enfield.

1913 Royal Enfield's own 350/425cc V-twin is the factory's first in-house motor.

1919 Enfield-Allday Bullet car shown at the London Motor Show and the 225cc two-stroke single goes on sale.

1923 Designer Ted Pardoe joins Royal Enfield and adds two single-cylinder 350 JAP-powered motorcycles to the range. The result is a total of eight models shown at London's Olympia Motorcycle Show.

1925 Royal Enfield announces that the JAP engines are to give way to four-stroke singles of Ted Pardoe's in-house design and Tony Wilson-Jones joins the firm.

1926 Royal Enfield expands the range with a 488cc side-valve model.

1930 Sloper single range announced and saddle tanks replace 'flat' tanks.

1932 Model Z Cycar on sale and the first use of the Bullet name on motorcycles.

1939 The baby Royal is shown, a lightweight that would become the wartime Flying Flea.

1941 Bradford-on-Avon factory established in stone quarries.

1948 The 350 Bullet is shown alongside the 500 Twin.

1952 The Bullet is now available as a 500 and the RE 125 becomes the 150 Ensign. Meteor 700 launched and 500 Twin evolves into the Meteor Minor.

1952 Order from the Indian Army for 350 Bullets for border patrol use.

1955 Bullet production starts in India.

1957 The first of the unit-construction 250 singles is shown, the Crusader.

1959 The Ensign is developed into the Prince and the Fury 500 is launched. A performance version of the Meteor is launched as the Constellation.

1962 Major Smith dies and E. & H.P. Smith (no relation) acquire Royal Enfield.

1963 The Series 1 Interceptor is launched.

1964 The 250cc Turbo Twin is almost all new, featuring a Villiers 2-cylinder, two-stroke motor. Geoff Duke joins Royal Enfield.

1965 The Continental GT 250 goes on sale and the GP5 racer is developed.

1967 Redditch works close, all production switched to Bradford-on-Avon.

1968 Series 2 Interceptor available.

1970 Production ceases at Bradford-on-Avon.

1989 Enfield India launches a 500 Bullet intended for export markets.

1994 Eicher group takes control of Enfield India.

1999 New all-alloy motor launched in the Bullet Machismo 350.

2001 Eicher wins the right in UK courts to the Royal Enfield.

2008 Unit construction singles on sale.

2017 The new 650 Royal Enfield Interceptor and Continental GT twins are unveiled.

2018 Concept KX bobber V-twin revealed.

2020 Single only available as a 350.

BEGINNINGS

According to Tripadvisor, the third best thing to do in Redditch is to visit the Forge Mill Needle Museum, pushed into the final podium spot behind the Arrow Valley Country Park and the Palace Theatre. Needle production was the genesis of what would become Royal Enfield, making Redditch its almost irresistible home. The town once produced some 90 per cent of the world's needles and the museum – once a needle factory – brings to life the sometimes gruesome story of needle making in Victorian times. It is also a reminder of how difficult life once was for most working people.

The first recorded mention of Redditch – probably simply derived from red ditch, the rubicund clay banks of local water courses and notably the River Arrow – dates from 1348 and the outbreak of the Black Death. During the Middle Ages Redditch became a centre of needle making, with factories powered by watermills. To this inventory was added fish hooks, fishing tackle and almost inevitably springs. The River Arrow also eventually flows into the River Avon, which in turn flows through Stratford-upon-Avon and on to the canal network, so accessing the rest of the country – and indeed the world in the days when waterways were the lifeblood of wealth creation and the British Empire. That there are five River Avons in England alone is simply explained. Avon is from an old Celtic word for river and the Welsh word for river is *afon*; yes, the River Avons are the River Rivers. The one that terminates at Bristol gave access to the most important port in the world after London. Heading north, the navigable waterways gave access to Liverpool, busy trying to push Bristol from the number two spot.

Little wonder then that Redditch was chosen by George Townsend when he set up a business making sewing needles in 1851. In 1882, his son, another George, added bicycle component manufacturing to the company's product range, including saddles and forks. By 1886, complete bicycles were being sold under the Townsend and Ecossais banner. Why a needle manufacturer expanded into cycles (meaning bicycles and tricycles, plus even quadricycles with four wheels) might seem odd from our perspective, cycles were one of the few growth areas in the economy when much of the world faced recession.

The Forge Mill Needle Museum, Redditch. The only water-powered scouring mill left in the world.
AMANDA SLATER

Inside the Forge Mill, giving an insight into factory working conditions at the time. There would only be modest improvement by the time the Redditch factory closed.
AMANDA SLATER

The UK's problems were precipitated by the Baring Crisis (also known as the Panic of 1890) and acute recession. Although less serious than some other financial crises of the era, it remains the nineteenth century's most famous sovereign debt crisis, brought on by the near insolvency of Barings Bank in London due principally to excessive risk-taking on poor investments in Argentina. Strikes in Australia and the United States were forerunners to an 1893 stock-market panic that led to recession in the USA and the Newfoundland Bank Crash of 1894, known then as Black Monday. More strikes and uncertainty followed, but the market for cycles almost alone bucked the trend, a front page of good news when every bulletin seemed to be relentlessly gloomy.

Cycling was revolutionized in August 1885 – the year in which Bianchi, still famous for its bicycles, was founded – when the safety bicycle was invented by John Kemp Starley. Characterized by two wheels of the same size, with a rear wheel driven by pedals below the saddle and a chain, it made for a more efficient bicycle that could use smaller wheels. The name came about because it was far easier to stay aboard than its predecessors, the Penny Farthing especially.

The low saddle, with easily reached pedals, allowed a more upright and controllable – so safer – seating position. This layout was quickly adapted to tricycles and quadricycles, and personal transport was born. Before the cycle, the only means of travel were with a horse – an impossible ambition for all but the wealthy and landed gentry – or by walking, where travel to the next town would typically take at least a day. For those who lived in villages or more rural settings, these cycles represented the first chance in history to meet more than the few hundred people who lived nearby.

This is why some have observed that the bicycle was the first 'Dating App': a chance to meet prospective partners beyond the handful available locally. In an era when people married very young the window of opportunity to meet a partner was realistically the few years between, say, thirteen or fourteen and one's early twenties. Inevitably the options would be few even in a larger town and mothers and vicars were seen as the only matchmakers. But bicycles allowed travel to towns in a few hours and there was suddenly the realistic possibility of attending a social gathering several miles away and being able to return to the parental home by nightfall.

In 1894, the so-called 'Betty Bloomers' became popular. These were effectively lightweight baggy trousers that could be worn under a skirt. Women were no longer limited to tricycles and could ride comfortably in their long skirts, powering the by now booming bicycle market. Demand was boosted further by the invention in 1887 of the pneumatic tyre. John Dunlop, a Scottish vet working with his brother James in Downpatrick, south of Belfast, first made pneumatic tyres for his child's tricycle before developing them for bicycle racing. He sold his rights for a modest sum, unaware how pivotal his invention would be, his only reward being a sort of immortality as his name remained when the Dunlop Rubber Company was established in 1901.

A 1902 Royal Enfield Girder model.
ONLINE BICYCLE MUSEUM

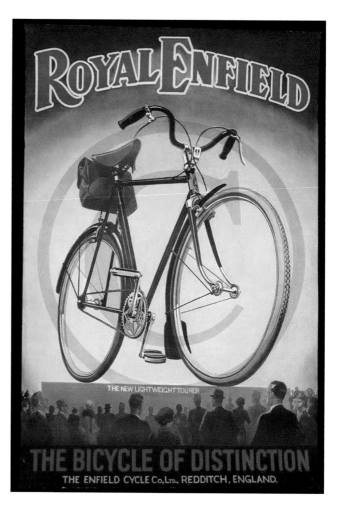

Bicycles were big business for Royal Enfield, but competition was fierce.

The second bottom frame rail was characteristic of the Royal Enfield Girder model. ONLINE BICYCLE MUSEUM

BANKRUPTCY AND REBIRTH

In economies where nothing seemed to be going well, bicycle or cycle part manufacture was adopted by everybody who had the necessary facilities. Despite this – or perhaps because there was so much competition – Townsend the bicycle and needle-making forerunner of Royal Enfield suffered financial collapse in 1891. By November of that year George Townsend's bankers settled on Albert Eadie, sales manager of Birmingham's Perry and Company, pen makers who had also started to make components for cycles, and Robert (known as Bob) Walker Smith, an engineer from D. Rudge and Company, to take over the business. So, in 1892, what would become Royal Enfield was reborn as the Eadie Manufacturing Company Limited, based in Snow Hill, Birmingham.

Despite Townsend being a well-respected needle manufacturer of almost fifty years' standing with a recent and unhappy adventure into bicycles, Eadie decided to diversify even further and chase government firearms contracts. The demand for guns had collapsed around 1860, driving the nascent Birmingham Small Arms (BSA) factory to near collapse, only saved by switching to bicycle manufacture. The only significant conflict by this time was the American Civil War, the Crimean War having ended in 1856. This would prove the fallibility of building a business's future around weaponry: there are times in history when wars are thankfully rare, but these are often unpredictable. Royal Enfield, like BSA, would have to find an alternative revenue stream and both would fall upon the same idea: the motorcycle. But before then there was to be a short-lived boom in firearms sales, as advances in rifle design led to a wholesale re-equipping of armies throughout the world.

The first British repeating rifle was developed in 1879. It was adopted as the Magazine Rifle Mark I in 1888 and was commonly referred to as the Lee-Metford. 'Lee' was James Paris Lee, a Scottish-born Canadian-American inventor who designed an easy to operate turn bolt and magazine to work with it. 'Metford' was William Ellis Metford, an Englishman instrumental in perfecting the smaller .303 calibre – the calibre of a Spitfire's Browning machine guns. These developments led to the Lee-Enfield repeating rifle that served as the British Empire and Commonwealth's main firearm during the first half of the twentieth century. It was also the British Army's standard rifle from its adoption in 1895 until 1957.

At some time in the early 1880s, suspecting their capacity to build enough guns in-house, the War Office promised the BSA gunsmiths free access to technical drawings and to the War Office's Board of Ordnance's Royal Small Arms factory at Enfield – hence Royal Enfield, although its connection to the Redditch factory of the same name was some way off. For now, the 'Royal Enfield' factory meant the government-owned facility close to London. New machinery developed in the United States had been installed at Enfield and greatly increased output without needing more skilled craftsmen. The great and the good of Birmingham viewed the expansion of Enfield with suspicion, knowing that the dedicated factory's proximity to London and long history of producing firearms gave it an advantage over the loose-knit gunsmiths of Birmingham, and so formed 'The BSA' to be sure of the capacity to compete.

Throughout the evolution of the British rifle the name Enfield is prevalent, but it originally referred to the Royal Small Arms Factory in the town – now suburb – of Enfield, just to the north-east of London. The British government had produced muskets since 1804 in this factory, but it had nothing like the capacity required to rearm a world desperate for the new Lee-Enfield repeating rifle. The British Empire's demand for rifles and ammunition rebounded from the 1860s slump to such an extent that eventually BSA abandoned bicycle and tricycle manufacture. The people at the top of BSA were gunsmiths and, in order to free factory floor space to build more Lee-Metford rifles, between 1888 and 1893 they returned BSA to its roots, turning production over entirely to the magazine rifle.

Albert Eadie and Bob Walker Smith decided that Eadie Manufacturing, based in Redditch just 15 miles (24km) or so south of BSA, decided to seize the opportunity and in 1893 this pair of entrepreneurs, trading under the Eadie banner, duly won a contract to supply precision parts to the Royal Small Arms Factory of Enfield, Middlesex. To celebrate this prestigious and lucrative order, they rechristened their undertaking the Enfield Manufacturing Company and launched their first Bob Walker Smith bicycle as the Enfield. Such was the extent of the estate of factories eventually covered that the Enfield name came to apply to the area rather than just the company. Indeed, even today, long after what became the Royal Enfield factories closed, maps of the region still carry the Enfield name.

Royal Enfield supplied guns and bicycles to the British army.
ROYAL ENFIELD

The "war" of 1913. The mobility of the silent bicycle enables its rider to cut the communications of the opposing force.

Lee-Metford Mark II .303. ARMÉMUSEUM/ SWEDISH ARMY MUSEUM

QUADRICYCLES 'MADE LIKE A GUN'

The following year, Eadie bicycles was renamed Royal Enfield and the trademark 'Made Like A Gun' was adopted. A motorcycle could not be far away, or so you might imagine. Instead, in 1898, the company launched a Walker Smith-designed motorized vehicle known as a Quadricycle built around two robust bicycle frames and powered by a proprietary 1½HP De Dion engine. The company also finalized its trading name as The Enfield Cycle Company Limited, a name it would use for the following seventy years.

In 1900, Royal Enfield entered one of its Quadricycles into the inaugural 1000 Mile Trial, following a tortuous cross-country route from London to Edinburgh and back. The inaugural London to Brighton Run in November 1896 may have been the birth of British motor sport, but by the end of the century there were still relatively few motorized vehicles on the roads, all seemingly owned and driven by apparently very rich people in flamboyant clothing. Indeed, the expression 'Gordon Bennett!' originates from the eponymous US publisher and motor-sport fan who sponsored the Gordon Bennett Cup in Europe. Most of the public had never seen a powered vehicle on the road and those who had were extremely shocked and frightened, being deeply suspicious of the bangs and unsilenced roar of the engines, let alone the dust kicked up as these monstrosities moved at great speed amongst the horse-drawn vehicles and pedestrians.

The Automobile Club of Great Britain was established in July 1897 (from 1907 it was known as the Royal Automobile Club, or RAC) to champion the car and the interests of all motorists, but several exhibitions and demonstrations had not gained support for the new mode of transport. And while the rest of the world seemed happy to accept motorcycle and automobile racing on open roads, Britain absolutely prohibited it. The general public disdain for the internal combustion engine was summed up by Kenneth Grahame's 1908 book, *The Wind in the Willows*, in which the wicked and feckless Toad obsesses about his motor car. Following the Motor Car Act of 1903, Britain was subject to a blanket 20mph (32km/h) speed limit, despite warnings that the embryonic British motor industry was being stifled at birth. Reliability and performance could not be developed while it remained illegal to go faster than 20mph and at one point the speed limit stood at 8mph (13km/h) in built-up areas and 12mph (19km/h) elsewhere. Thus the 'British' Gordon Bennett Cup of 1903 was held in Athy, a market town in County Kildare in the Republic of Ireland, some 50 miles (80km) south-west of Dublin. In gratitude to the Irish, the British team painted its car in a shamrock green livery and created 'British' Racing Green. The ban is also the reason that Surrey landowner Hugh Locke King opened Brooklands on 17 June 1907, the first purpose-built motor racing circuit in the world.

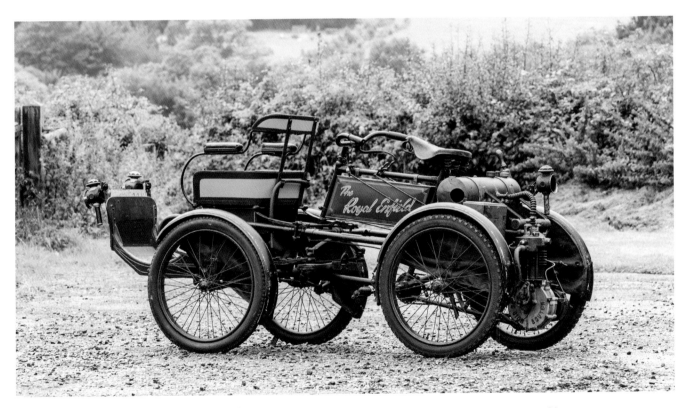

The first powered Royal Enfield, the Quadricycle, basically two bicycles and an engine powered by a French De Dion single-cylinder motor. BONHAMS

Rear view of the Quadricycle. Works manager, Bob Walker Smith, designed the prototype for his own use. Seating the driver over the engine and behind the passenger, it closely followed the lines of the popular De Dion 'quad'. The single-cylinder motor displaced 244cc and gave a maximum speed of 30mph (48km/h). BONHAMS

Unsurprisingly, given these restrictions the British motor industry did not progress as quickly as the French, Belgian and German equivalents over the next few years. In the summer of 1899, the Automobile Club Secretary, Claude Johnson, conceived the idea of a trial, with a series of daily runs of up to 100 miles (161km) that would test a driver's patience and skill, but more importantly the design, construction and reliability of the cars. There would also be exhibitions in the main towns along the way, to try to convince the population of the pleasures and reliability of powered transport and so overcome prejudice.

The original 1000 Mile Trial of 1900 started in Grosvenor Place in London and followed a route through Bristol, Birmingham, Manchester, Derby, Kendal, Carlisle, Edinburgh, Newcastle, Leeds, Sheffield, Nottingham and back to London. There were eighty-three entries originally, although only sixty-five actually made the start. By Edinburgh, fifty-one were still running, but, in the end, only thirty-five vehicles made it back to London. The itinerary ran from 23 April to 12 May and comprised eleven days of driving between 61 and 122 miles (98 and 196km), the final total distance being 1,060 miles (1,706km). There were four hill-climb competitions and an optional speed trial, with various exhibitions along the way.

In the quaint terminology of the time, motoring was referred to as 'the field of automobilism', owners and drivers were either 'automobilists' or 'autocarists' and mechanics were known as 'mechanicians'. The vehicles were open to the weather and, even if some had a canvas hood, there were no windscreens so that 'automobilists' had to be suitably dressed in 'autocoats', hats and goggles. The event is still run occasionally today by the Historic Endurance Rallying Organisation (HERO).

The 1000 Mile Trial was a resounding success and, despite the insistence of some drivers on 'taking liqueurs with lunch', the only casualties were an unfortunate dog and an 'unmanageable' horse. It was an historic moment in the popularization of the car: 'Quite simply, it put motoring on the map,' says Ben Cussons, chairman of the Motoring Committee of the Royal Automobile Club. The Royal Enfield Quadricycle was one of the thirty-five finishers and, despite its share of difficulties and breakdowns, was awarded a silver medal. Little wonder that Enfield initially decided its future lay with four wheelers.

THE FIRST ROYAL ENFIELD MOTORCYCLE

Despite the initial commitment to cars, the first Royal Enfield motorcycle was finally built in 1901. Again a design from the pen of Bob Walker Smith aided by Frenchman Jules Gotiet, it had a 1½HP Minerva engine mounted in front of the steering head. Although this meant that the motor was above the front wheel, it was the rear wheel that was driven

by a long rawhide belt. Beyond this, little is known – or at least certain – about the motorcycle. Most of the images are drawings and sources claim the Minerva single-cylinder four-stroke motor variously as 150cc, 172cc and even a 239cc upgrade with innovations such as a spray carburettor and battery and coil ignition, attributed to French designer Louis Goviet. Mick Walker's book, entitled *Royal Enfield – The Complete Story* (also published by Crowood), perhaps wisely doesn't even mention the size of the motor.

Minerva had started out manufacturing bicycles in 1897, before in 1900 expanding into light cars and motorized bicycles. Back then, Belgium was at the forefront of the internal combustion engine's development, but its head start was destroyed by World War I. The company took its name from the Roman goddess of wisdom and strategy, but she was also the sponsor of arts and – most importantly – trade. The company produced lightweight clip-on engines that mounted below the bicycle front down-tube, specifically for Minerva bicycles but also available in kit form that

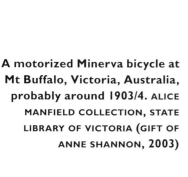

A motorized Minerva bicycle at Mt Buffalo, Victoria, Australia, probably around 1903/4. ALICE MANFIELD COLLECTION, STATE LIBRARY OF VICTORIA (GIFT OF ANNE SHANNON, 2003)

Royal Enfield's first motorcycle, 1901, with a Minerva engine. A HERL INC

was suitable for almost any bicycle. The engine drove a belt turning a large gear wheel attached to the side of the rear wheel opposite to the chain. In 1901, the kit engine was a 211cc unit, allowing comfortable cruising at around 20mph (32km/h) and half as much again on full throttle.

In these pioneering days the horsepower rating was not as universal as it is today, where the quoted brake horsepower (bhp) is a measure of an engine's ability to turn a brake of some sort. While this empirical measurement was available to engineers from the birth of the internal combustion engine, British tax authorities at least insisted on a theoretical calculation based upon the engine's specification, determined by the RAC in the UK. This equated 1HP as equal to 2sq in (12.9sq cm) of piston area and came to be known as the Treasury Rating. Perhaps even more oddly, manufacturers would list models by this rating rather than give them a name. It was the 1930s before this changed and even the

fabulous Coventry Eagle Flying Eight was thus named after its RAC 8HP rating, despite producing around 30bhp.

So while Minerva claimed 1.5HP at 1,500rpm, the motor was rated at 2HP or 2.25HP in the UK. These kits to turn bicycles into powered two-wheelers were exported as far as Australia. Minerva struggled to build on its early success, hampered – hammered even – by two world wars and the Depression, but it was still making Land Rovers under licence for the Belgium Army as late as 1956.

Then, in 1902, Triumph launched its first motorcycle, expanding rapidly from bicycle production with funding from Dunlop tyres. The vehicle was an immediate hit, powered by a single-cylinder four-stroke Minerva engine with automatic inlet valve and battery/coil ignition, clipped to the down tube of a Triumph bicycle frame.

Triumph sold 500 of its Minerva-powered motorcycles in 1903 and started prototyping with British JAP (John Alfred

Prestwich) motors for an expanded range. The same year, BSA experimented with a motorcycle with a BSA pattern frame fitted with a Minerva 233cc engine, similar to the contemporary Triumph's, although BSA would launch its own motorcycle with an engine designed and built in-house. These would be the leading lights of the embryonic British (English, in reality) motorcycle manufacturers, although Royal Enfield initially decided that motor cars would be its future. The motor department was put into a separate subsidiary, Enfield Autocar Company Limited, which was incorporated in 1906 and established in new works at Hunt End, although still in Redditch. However, after just nineteen months Enfield Autocar reported substantial losses and, apart from Albert Eadie himself, shareholders were unwilling to provide more capital.

In early 1907, Eadie therefore sold his control of Eadie Manufacturing to BSA. Albert Eadie and Bob Walker Smith were promised that they would be appointed directors of BSA before the proposed sale (in truth a takeover, largely funded by offering BSA shares to Eadie stakeholders) was put to shareholders. The new combined BSA and Eadie business was incorporated to manufacture 'military and sporting rifles, [pedal] cycle and cycle components, motor-cars *et cetera*', noting that these were BSA and Eadie specialities, Eadie cycle parts being almost as famous as BSA's at the

time. Years later, the BSA chairman would tell shareholders that the acquisition had 'done wonders for the cycle department'. Ironically, Eadie was allowed a separate identity when Raleigh bought BSA's bicycle interests in 1957 when there were still minority Eadie shareholders alongside BSA's.

THE FIRST REDDITCH BULLET

This would prove to be a BSA trait, buying up the local competition. In 1910, BSA would acquire the Daimler Motor Company, just as BSA was about to enter the motorcycle business. But it left the business of Enfield Autocar, which amounted to little more than plant and stock, to be sold to Birmingham's Alldays and Onions Pneumatic Engineering. The Enfield Cycle Company took over the Hunt End premises that had been acquired to establish Enfield Autocar. The twist here is that this is the trail that leads to the Bullet name first being used: Alldays and Onions had, in 1898, produced its first car cum quadricycle, the Traveller, although series production did not start until 1903/4. But the first real commercial success came with the 1.6-litre, vertical-twin side-valve 10/12 (indicating horsepower tax ratings), made from 1905 to 1913. It was popular with commercial drivers and did well in period formula events and hill climbs.

The Enfield-Allday Bullet, the first Enfield to carry the Bullet name, although only a handful of prototypes were made. This chassis was shown at the 1919 Olympia Show. A HERL INC

This **BSA** outfit was the sort of personal transport that even affluent families aspired to, and cost half what a car might.
BONHAMS

Following the takeover of Enfield Autocar, the Enfield-designed cars were phased out before the war, leaving them as badge-engineered Alldays. Post-war, the business became Enfield-Allday Motors based in Sparkbrook, with all previous models dropped in favour of a new 10HP car called the Enfield-Allday Bullet. This, the first Enfield to carry the Bullet name, had an air-cooled, 5-cylinder, sleeve-valve, radial engine of 1247cc mounted at the front of a tubular steel lattice frame. Drive was to the rear wheels via shaft, first to a central three-speed gearbox and then on to the rear axle. Suspension was by transverse cantilever springs. A three-seat body was offered at a price of £295, although by the time the car was exhibited in 1919 at the London Motor Show this had risen to £350.

Even so, this still looked unbelievable value for a car. The 1921 771cc BSA Model E V-twin, when matched to BSA's own matching green and cream painted sidecar, retailed at half that price and was almost as powerful at 7HP. Even that was a lot of money when £4 a week was a decent wage, but a comparative bargain when the basic Austin Twenty car cost £595.

So it was little surprise when A.C. 'Gus' Bertelli of the Grahame-White Aviation Company was called in for advice on the Enfield-Allday Bullet. He reported that a lot of development was still required and that the proposed price would make the car woefully uneconomic to produce. He eventually suggested that the car would need to retail at some £550. This was too much for the market to bear and perhaps only five Enfield-Allday Bullets reached customers. It was hardly an auspicious start to what would be an illustrious history for the Enfield Bullet moniker.

Royal Enfield, however, was now a name and a factory in need of a product, with the armoury and bicycle business gone to BSA and the cars to Alldays and Onion. The Enfield Cycle Company remained well known and an important source of revenue for decades to come, including in-house designed and manufactured brakes and hubs sold to other bicycle and motorcycle builders. Royal Enfield would even make frames for the famous Scott two-stroke twins, so it was hardly a surprise when the company started buying in engines to build its own complete motorcycles.

2

THE V-TWINS

Royal Enfield stunned all comers at Milan's EICMA 2018 Motorcycle Show by unveiling the Concept KX – a modern reimagining of the 1930s Royal Enfield V-twin on the right. ROYAL ENFIELD

Anybody who thinks that the V-twins are just a footnote in Royal Enfield's history, or a pre-war curiosity best left to fans of flying helmets and goggles, would do well to note which motorcycle the company's CEO, Siddhartha Lal, loves best:

> *Of all the models in Enfield's history the KX [1930s V-twin] is my favourite. It's from such a fascinating time in motorcycling history. It was before the English*

and American markets split into parallel twins and cruisers, so it has style elements that we would associate with both. My personal favourite part is the tank; there are no other shapes like it out there.

That Siddhartha Lal said this at the time of the launch of the Interceptor and Continental GT 650 parallel twins suggests that these are far from the limit of the Indian factory's ambitions, especially with these models providing an important bridgehead to the lucrative US market, which was never going to fall in love with modest four-stroke single-cylinder motorcycles. Just how ambitious Royal Enfield is was further hinted at in late 2018 when it stunned all comers at Milan's EICMA Motorcycle Show by unveiling the Concept KX – a modern re-imagining of the 1930s Royal Enfield V-twin and proof that the factory understands its heritage and potential. They have a fine history of building V-twins, which, oddly enough, starts in Switzerland.

COLLABORATION WITH MOTOSACOCHE AND A RETURN TO MOTORCYCLES

Royal Enfield's first V-twin, using a 297cc Swiss-made Motosacoche engine, was first shown at the 1909 Stanley Cycle Show held from 19 to 27 November. This was the thirty-third of these important shows, which had expanded

from their cycling origins to embrace motoring and were by then held at the Royal Agricultural Hall, Islington, in London.

Founded in Geneva in 1899, Motosacoche (pronounced 'moto sa-cosh') took its name from Henri and Armand Dufaux's self-contained cyclemotor, literally 'moto sac-oche' (motor [in a small] bag). The first 211cc four-stroke single was sold from 1900 to be fitted to bicycle frames, following swiftly in Minerva's footsteps. It was soon being manufactured in substantial numbers and the brothers set up a subsidiary company to market it in the UK, first through H. and A. Dufaux England Limited and then, by 1912, Motosacoche Limited (Great Britain), with Osborne Louis De Lissa. Motosacoche quickly grew to have factories in Switzerland, France and Italy, and supplied engines badged as MAG (Motosacoche Acacias Genève, Acacias being a commune within Geneva) to continental manufacturers including Clement, Condor, Imperia, Neander and Monet Goyon. This led to the collaboration with Royal Enfield, which supplied the cycle parts to create a complete Motosacoche motorcycle and inevitably led to

An early Motosacoche motorcycle from a family and holiday album, 1899–1908. PHOTOGRAPHED BY ARTHUR D.WHITLING FROM THE COLLECTION OF THE STATE LIBRARY OF NEW SOUTH WALES

Motosacoche A1 from 1904. KLAUS NAHR

Motosacoche V-twin power when Royal Enfield recommenced motorcycle production itself. The 1910 Royal Enfield used a Motosacoche 344cc 2.75HP inlet-over-exhaust (IOE) V-twin, also reputed to have been supplied to Triumph, Ariel, Matchless and Brough Superior.

The Motosacoche and Royal Enfield ranges were effectively identical for the first few years, but after World War I the Swiss marque's presence in the UK was limited to supplying the proprietary MAG engines to other manufacturers. These highly regarded Swiss power plants were widely used, the French and Italian markets being served by subsidiary factories in Lyon and Milan respectively. A Motosacoche won the inaugural 1922 Bol d'Or. Motosacoche's characteristic IOE engines were largely replaced by side-valve versions towards the end of the 1920s, while for sports and competition a range of overhead valve (ohv) and even overhead camshaft (ohc) cylinder heads were available. These were designed by, among others, Dougal Marchant and the famous Bert Le Vack, who was killed while testing a

new model in 1931. Post-World War II, Motosacoche was a shadow of its former self, producing a very limited range and ceasing motorcycle production in 1957.

ROYAL ENFIELD'S FIRST V-TWIN

The demise of the Enfield Autocar company in 1908 followed an oversupply in the car market as new players piled in against a background of rising unemployment. However, the rapidly improving British motorcycle market tempted Royal Enfield to try its luck once more with two-wheelers. William Guillon – who was either Swiss or French, but probably the former – was an engineer late of the Belgian FN concern (another guns to motorcycles business) and had been offered a post under Bob Walker Smith to assist in the design and development of cars initially, alongside Harry Lancaster. But Walker Smith then saw Guillon pen a motorcycle, the result being first shown at the 1909 Stanley

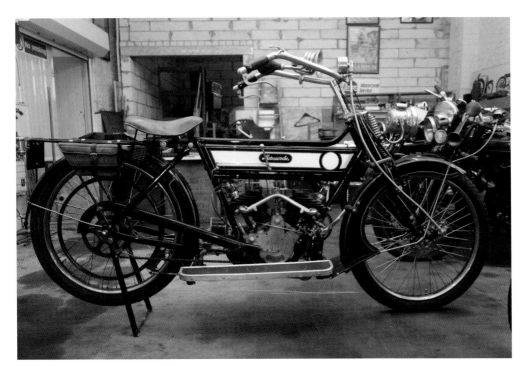

A 2CV7 496cc V-twin Motosacoche, c. 1914. Note that the engines were by now badged as **MAG**.

This 1911 Royal Enfield 2¾HP Model 160 has the Motosacoche 344cc inlet IOE V-twin. The family likeness to the **MAG** unit in the previous image is obvious. BONHAMS

Cycle Show for deliveries commencing in 1910. In a some-what questionable statement, the show bike is sometimes described as side valve rather than Motosacoche's usual IOE layout, but these may be genuine differences. These were easy and comparatively minor mistakes to make, given that the internal combustion engine was still in its infancy and motor vehicles remained largely bespoke. The production Royal Enfield V-twin was listed as the Model 150 and came with the 297cc Motosacoche 2¼HP V-twin, with fixed-ratio belt drive, magneto ignition, a hand pump for lubrication and front forks with what was described as a 'Druid' pattern, a trade name that became as generic as Hoover did for vacuum cleaners. Druid girder-style forks are side sprung (that is, have two springs). Enfield only used Druid forks for the 1910 season and for 1911 they were all designed and made by Enfield and marketed as such.

Metalwork was apparently painted a shade of khaki, although this may be a faded green compared to the appearance on delivery. And of course, they were 'made like a gun': it's surprising that BSA never challenged that.

For the following season – 1911 – 2¾HP was claimed, with the 344cc motor. This was dubbed the Model 160 and offered all chain drive and Enfield's admired two-speed gearbox, effectively a choice of primary drive chains. There was also the option of cush drive, a first on a British motorcycle. The rear wheel hub had a second hub within it, the two joined by a series of radial rubber blocks or vanes, making for gentler getaways, gear changes and much reduced wear on the drive chains. Royal Enfield historian and creator of The Vintage Motor Cycle Club's (VMCC) Banbury Run put it thus: 'This was a very peculiar type of hub which contained about six rubber blocks which very gently took up the drive instead of having to snatch on it which you normally have to get off a chain and a solid back tyre.'

The Model 160 would remain listed until 1914, by which time it cost £45. This was cheaper than the BSA 3½HP single priced at £50, also available with a 'free' engine, referring to the double cone clutch in the rear hub, at £56 10s. To put these prices in perspective, in 1910 average annual earnings were around £70 for men and £30 for women working a 55-hour week.

H. Greaves rode a 2¼HP Royal Enfield V-twin in the July 1910 Auto-Cycle Union (ACU, Britain's motorcycle sport ruling body) Land's End to John O'Groats Trial, completing the run without losing points. Greaves, together with Royal Navy Lieutenant H.T. Bennett and P. Islip, entered their

Enfields. Greaves and Islip had non-stop runs and Greaves won a gold medal. Lieutenant Bennett unfortunately had an accident and did not finish. Islip and Greaves entered the October ACU trials and had non-stop runs. There were also gold medals for Enfield riders in the Six Days' Trial – something that was going to become an Enfield event of choice – and two gold medals in the Edinburgh to London reliability trial towards the end of the year.

But the Land's End event was halted in 1911, with Ivan B. Hart-Davies becoming the holder of the final Land's End to John O'Groats record for solo motorcycles. Riding his 3½HP single-speed Triumph, he covered the 886 miles (1,426 km) in 29 hours, 12 minutes. But, as his average speed exceeded the then-speed limit of 20mph (32km/h), further official record attempts were banned by the ACU.

KEEPING IT IN THE FAMILY

Another important development in 1910 was that Frank Smith, the eldest son of Bob Walker Smith, joined Royal Enfield. He was twenty-one years old, had studied at Quinton College and Birmingham University and been apprenticed at BSA. Frank (later Major) Smith would eventually run the entire business until his death in 1962, an event, compounded by the death in 1963 of Major Mountford, that some claim provoked the decline of Royal Enfield during the second half of the 1960s. Mountford had joined Royal Enfield in the 1950s, becoming sales manager before replacing Smith on his death as joint managing director, alongside former racing star Leo Davenport. But that is half a century away from this part of the story and the expansion of Royal Enfield's V-twin ambitions, which necessitated moving on from Motosacoche to JAP engines.

JAP was engineer John Alfred Prestwich, who started out making scientific instruments in 1895, aged just twenty, initially behind his father's house at 1 Lansdowne Road, Tottenham, in London. By 1911, he had moved to new premises in Tariff Road, in the Northumberland Park area of Tottenham. Prestwich was initially best known for his cinematography cameras and projectors, working with Z de Ferranti and later the cinema pioneer William Friese-Greene.

In about 1902, JAP started the business for which it is best remembered, the manufacture of motorcycle engines used in many famous motorcycle marques, most notably Brough Superior. Some claim that Royal Enfield's first motorcycle

Royal Enfield had this new 3HP solo for 1913, powered by its own 425cc IOE engine. BONHAMS

This is a 1914 version, still a 3HP 425cc V-twin, although it was raced successfully in 350cc form at Brooklands and the Isle of Man TT. BONHAMS

This 1913 Model 180 has the 6HP 770cc JAP V-twin. BONHAMS

had a JAP motor, although, given its 1901 appearance it almost certainly predates JAP's first power unit. Even after World War II, JAP's motorcycle engines continued to be associated with racing and record success, and were still used in speedway bikes well into the 1960s.

So it was with the already famous JAP V-twin 770cc side-valve motor that Royal Enfield's 6HP Model 180, supplied as a sidecar outfit, joined the range for 1912. The Redditch factory continued the V-twin theme with a new Model 140 3HP solo for 1913, now powered by Enfield's own 425cc IOE V-twin that had been prototyped at 344cc in 1912 and was the factory's first in-house motor. This was rated at 2¾HP, with an unusual cylinder head architecture, an overhead inlet valve and a side exhaust valve. There was also a ladies' version with an open frame that allowed it to be ridden wearing a skirt. Royal Enfield had now established a reputation for being technically adventurous, adopting multi-speed transmission, chain drive, automatic dry-sump lubrication – a solid decade ahead of the competition and astounding in an era when riders were usually expected to accommodate an engine's lubrication needs with a hand-operated oil pump – and the patented cush-drive rear hub that would remain a feature of all future models until the 1960s.

RACING ROYAL ENFIELD'S NEW V-TWIN

The factory had already raced Motosacoche-powered Royal Enfields with Bert Colver at the TT in July 1911 and at Brooklands in August the same year. Colver had ridden at the TT in 1909 and 1910 for Matchless, winners of the inaugural TT singles race in 1907. He failed to finish any races on the island for Enfield and would return to Matchless for 1914, but won his class at Brooklands' British Motor Cycle Racing Club (BMCRC, founded in 1909) in August 1911 covering 54 miles 122yd (87km 112m) in an hour. His 2¾HP V-twin had an odd two-part fuel tank with the magneto between them, rigid forks, as was the norm for racers, and an unusual all-chain drive. Meanwhile, Enfield's other rider, Greaves, who had won a gold medal with the factory in the July 1910 Land's End to John O'Groats Trial, finished fifth in the 1911 TT. This was the first year that the Mountain course had been used for the TT and several manufacturers complained that it was too testing on machinery and threatened to boycott the 1912 races.

But Enfield returned in 1913 to the Isle of Man, with new in-house engines in a new frame, plus the now famous glass oil tank. The racers were still 344cc, the capacity of the

Bert Colver in 1911, with a Royal Enfield 2¾HP V-racer, with an odd two-part fuel tank with the magneto between them. Rigid forks were the norm for racers, but it is unusual to see all-chain drive.

The Concours d'Endurance in Marly-le-Roi (a town east of Paris) on 24 April 1921. This was a long-distance event, organized by the Union Motocycliste de France. On the right is M. Oblin, with M. Vernillet. Oblin was a regular competitor in events on his Royal Enfield outfit with Diane sidecar.
A HERL INC

prototype and within the Junior TT's 350cc maximum permitted capacity. With the road bike (the Model 140 3HP twin) at 425cc, it is likely that the 344cc version was sleeved down, as photos show crankcases with a bulge at the base of the cylinders on the primary drive side, a feature of the 425cc cases. The magneto also moved to the front of the engine, allowing the fuel tank to be a full-length, one-piece item of greater capacity, a worthwhile advantage in the long TT races.

Enfield took five riders to the Isle of Man for the 1913 races, but only two finished (Greaves and C.M. Down in lowly seventeenth and sixteenth places respectively); Colver, D.S. Alexander and Ernest Keyte (known as 'Bones' for his skinny frame) were all DNFs (Did Not Finish). For 1914, they remained unbowed, returning with a team of nine riders and almost scooping the win, although instead the Junior TT ended in tragedy. Yet of the nine riders only F.E. Wasling failed to finish and Frank Walker was posthumously awarded third place.

With war clouds gathering, the 1914 TT races were remembered as the event in which the big thumping singles fought back in their constant battle with the twin-cylinder machines. Following the two fatal accidents the previous year, crash helmets were made compulsory and the start line was moved to the top of Bray Hill, close to where it is today.

The Junior (for motors up to 350cc) TT had been reduced from six to five laps, but still a race distance of around 185 miles (298km) and was held in terrible conditions. Heavy rain and mist on the Mountain Course gave competitors a hard time, although it did produce a tremendous race. Leading the singles' charge was the AJS team, its motorcycles featuring twin primary chains and a two-speed countershaft, allowing four-speed gear selection. Their riders Eric Williams and Cyril Williams (no relation) eventually finished first and second respectively, having constantly swapped the lead with the V-twin Royal Enfield and flat-twin Douglas motorcycles.

But the excitement of the race was marred by the tragic death of Frank Walker, who had been leading on his Royal Enfield until he had a puncture on the third lap. Such was the fury of his pursuit of the two leading AJays that he led twice more during the race, but, at the finish, whether because he was so exhausted he had lost count of the number of laps or simply because he could not stop, he crashed into the wooden pole placed across the track to signify the race was over and was fatally injured.

Hard as it is to believe today, the introduction of a V-twin was lauded as an innovation. In *The Motor Cycle and Cycle Trader* of 17 March 1916, tester Mr Paskell said that there had hardly been any bike introduced in the UK that did not copy Triumph and BSA's lead in adopting single-cylinder engines. 'Almost the only notable exception which did not join the rank for the 3½HP single is the Enfield, due perhaps to the independent "never follow anyone" style of a man, that mechanical genius, R.W. Smith.'

WAR AND A STORY OF REMARKABLE COURAGE

That the Model 140 was still being written about in 1916 tells that Royal Enfield's innovation was, like most others, subsumed by World War I and the need to furnish the war effort rather than private buyers. There was, however, a new two-stroke, the 1915 Model 200, a 225cc two-stroke lightweight engine that we will revisit in Chapter 3. Other than that, Royal Enfield carried on with its V-twins, increasing production, usually with a sidecar and often with a machine gun mounted on the sidecar, as their part of the war effort. From 1914, Royal Enfield supplied large numbers of motorcycles to the British War Department and also won a motorcycle contract for the Imperial Russian Government. The V-twins also went to the Belgian, French and US armies, usually the 3HP smaller V-twins designed and built in-house. The focus for the British was on 6HP and 8HP motorcycle sidecar models fitted with the big JAP V-twin and a Vickers machine gun based on the earlier Maxim. Some were alternatively fitted out as an 'ambulance' (in reality a stretcher on the sidecar chassis), but the bulk of production was given over to bicycles at a rate of 500 a week, still an important and sizeable part of Royal Enfield's output even when the world was not at war.

Throughout the war years Enfield continued to innovate, experimenting with a 675cc 3-cylinder in-line two-stroke, based on the 225cc single, with a bevel drive to a two-speed gearbox then to the rear wheel by chain. Later came an 848cc in-line side-valve 4 of unit construction with a three-speed gearbox. Neither went into production, although the triple was registered with the number ABP4 in 1934. It is now in the National Motorcycle Museum in Solihull.

Royal Enfield 976cc
JAP V-twin powered
outfit with Diane
sidecar; Oblin again
during the 1920
Paris–Nice race.
A HERL INC

Another view of Enfield's own
425cc V-twin in the 1914 3HP
solo. BONHAMS

Remarkably, the in-line 4 also survives in the National Motor Museum in Beaulieu, Hampshire.

Royal Enfield also had a small part to play in one of the greatest tales told during World War I. When they met at a motorcycle club in 1912, Elsie Knocker was a

The two-stroke triple prototype in the National Motorcycle Museum.

The 1919 Royal Enfield Experimental, with the side-valve 4-cylinder motor in the National Motor Museum in Beaulieu. PRZEMYSŁAW JAHR

thirty-year-old motorcycling divorcee dressed in bottle-green Dunhill leathers and Mairi Chisholm was a brilliant eighteen-year-old mechanic, living at home and borrowing tools from her brother. Little did they know, but theirs was to become one of the most extraordinary stories of the conflict among the trenches.

Elsie had trained as a nurse and was a long-time rider who would take Mairi to the front line in her Chater-Lea's sidecar. Mairi had learned to ride on her brother's Royal Enfield. They had met roaring around West Country lanes competing in motorcycle and sidecar trials and, in 1914, roared off to London to 'do their bit'. When they turned up at Victoria station in leather breeches, boots and overcoats the other women volunteers were horrified. Yet Elsie and Mairi were described as 'larky in khaki' by their biographer and within a few weeks they were living and working on the fighting front – the only women to do so – in Belgium, driving ambulances to distant military hospitals. Frustrated by the number of men dying of shock – usually meaning blood loss – in the back of their vehicles, they set up their own first-aid post in the village of Pervyse, a hundred yards or so from Ypres front line, risking their lives working under sniper fire and heavy bombardment for months at a time. But risking their lives saved many others and established what paramedics now call the 'golden hour', stabilizing the wounded before they were moved to a hospital.

The pair lived and worked in 'cellar houses' – bombed-out ruins with spacious or at least adequate cellars – where the conditions were appalling, with headroom usually less than 6ft (1.8m) – 'spacious' was a relative term. The Germans came to admire them and their commanding officer agreed that if they wore white nursing caps when rescuing the wounded they would not be shot at. This was heroism of the highest order, all the more impressive given that they were unpaid and had to return often to England to raise funds.

But their fame began to spread, with newspaper articles and meetings with the good and great. Harrods donated a steel outer door to secure their cellar house, painted with a large red cross on it. King Albert of Belgium awarded them the Knights Order of Leopold II and their legend spread as 'The Madonnas of Pervyse'. In the end, they were among just seventeen women awarded the Military Medal during the war.

Although almost forgotten now, Elsie Knocker and Mairi Chisholm became celebrities in their day, visited by journalists and photographers as well as royals. Glamorous and influential, they were having the time of their lives and, for almost four years, Elsie and Mairi stayed in Pervyse until they were almost killed by arsenic gas in the spring of 1918. Returning home and adjusting to peacetime life was to prove even more challenging than the war itself. The picture of them on a Royal Enfield 6HP sidecar outfit is from a film, supervised by legendary director D.W. Griffith, that was used for fundraising purposes during the war.

Where the world was not consumed by war, Royal Enfield's reputation continued to grow. Even before hostilities flared, the new V-twin Enfield did well overseas. A Mr Flowers and passenger claimed to ride one to Mount Olympus from Cairo and competition success included a win in the 300-mile (483km) Indian TT race from Calcutta to Gaya over very difficult roads. The 2.75HP also won the Bloemfontein Hill Climb in South Africa and the Svenska MK Reliability Trial – and everything else – in Sweden. In 1915, the little V-twin won King Alphonse's Cup in the Spanish International Motor Cycle Trial, something that would become part of the International Six Day Trials (ISDT), in which Royal Enfield would come to shine. Further afield

still, a 3HP won the Canberra Motor Cycling Club's 10-mile (16km) race at an average of 54mph (87km/h) in 1913 and by 1916 the country's *Wheeling* magazine declared that 'there are few motorcycles better known in Australia and New Zealand than the Royal Enfield machines'.

Back at home, Royal Enfield could not keep up with demand, despite expansion of premises and reacquiring the Givvy works at Hunt End. Despite working at full capacity and introducing night shifts, by 1915 the company had back orders for 2,000 motorcycles from private buyers. To be fair, the press was reporting lead times for motorcycle deliveries of eight to twelve weeks as fuel shortages drove buyers away from cars to motorcycles, including a number of police forces.

World War I fuel rationing saw the Enfield become the machine of choice for those looking to run their bike on coal gas, often trailered behind a 6HP sidecar outfit in a huge balloon. One lady enthusiast had her gasbag fitted to a large tray above the occupants' heads and whilst the engine power was reported as being unchanged, the same could not be said for the aerodynamics of such transport.

British ambulance drivers Elsie Knocker, the Baroness de T'Serclaes, and Mairi Chisholm ('The Madonnas of Pervyse') in the ruins of Pervyse, 30 July 1917.
GEORGE GRANTHAM BAIN COLLECTION (LIBRARY OF CONGRESS) PHOTOGRAPHER LIEUTENANT ERNEST BROOKS

Nurses Mairi Chisholm and Elsie Knocker both loved motorcycles and pioneered front-line care. The Royal Enfield outfit was supplied for a fundraising film in Pervyse, 7 September 1917. GEORGE GRANTHAM BAIN COLLECTION (LIBRARY OF CONGRESS)

The Madonnas of Pervyse again in Pervyse, 30 July 1917. GEORGE GRANTHAM BAIN COLLECTION (LIBRARY OF CONGRESS) PHOTOGRAPHER LIEUTENANT ERNEST BROOKS

This demand for Royal Enfield's products led to a boom in wages and profits, which rose to around £33,000 per annum in 1914 and would reach almost £72,000 by 1918. Despite Enfield's board issuing statements denying any profiteering, perhaps unsurprisingly the British government acted. From summer 1915, Royal Enfield became one of the government's 'controlled assets', meaning that the company could only supply the war effort. Then in 1918 an Excess Profit Duty and Munitions Levy took more than £11,000 from the profits. There was also a wartime conundrum in that, somehow, Royal Enfield maintained its relationship with Motosacoche in Switzerland. In 1918, a number of sidecar rolling chassis were dispatched to Geneva, even featuring Royal Enfield's cutting-edge cush hubs. One can only guess that they were shipped out without the JAP engine for Motosacoche to install its own. How all this happened during the war when the factory was under government control is something of a mystery.

Royal Enfield survived the war in good shape. Joint managing directors and father and son Bob and Frank Smith also survived, despite Frank serving as a pilot in the Royal Flying Corps, rising to Major – the name he would be known by – as he fought in France. His two younger brothers also came through the war and this allowed a stability that would serve Royal Enfield well, as would the three siblings' shared love of off-roading.

A RETURN TO CIVILIAN LIFE

Yet a return to normal civilian life was not without problems 'of reconstruction', as Bob Smith put it: 'My opinion is that this will best be met by producing existing models for the immediate future so that there will be the least possible delay in delivery.' Civilian models returned in 1919, but in just two forms. The only option Smith would countenance was swapping the side of the hand gear shift if the prospective buyer had been injured in conflict and could not ride the motorcycle as delivered. Otherwise there were no options or variations and the only models available were the 6HP JAP V-twin with an 8HP engine option for sidecar work and the 225cc two-stroke sold as basic transport. For 1921, the 8HP engine was replaced with a 976cc V-twin Wolseley motor made by Vickers to an Enfield design specifically for this model. This was a completely new large-displacement motorcycle, mainly for the important sidecar business. The engine was started with a large hand crank beneath the solo saddle, a nod to the Vickers' aircraft-engine origins. As the Royal Enfield was designed as a touring machine, there were large footboards for the comfort of any size of rider and the front and rear mudguards were designed to keep as much water and filth from the rider and sidecar passenger as possible; this would also protect the forward-mounted magneto from drowning in water spray. Throttle, choke and

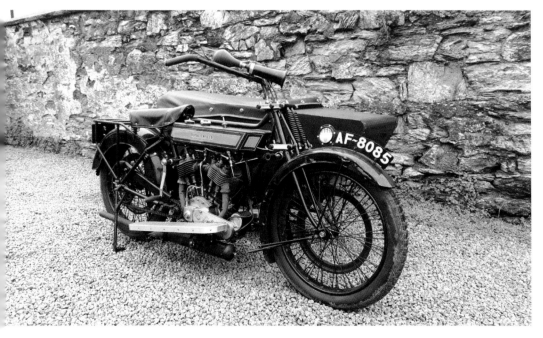

When motorcycle production resumed after World War I, the Enfield combination reappeared with an 8HP JAP engine, though this was soon superseded by one of Enfield's own design, manufactured by Vickers. Displacing 976cc, the 8HP engine had been redesigned and was being built at Enfield's Redditch works by 1925, at which time the three-speed Sturmey-Archer gearbox and hand clutch were adopted for all models except the two-stroke lightweight. BONHAMS

air controls were all by finger levers. Only two of these machines are known to have survived.

Enfield then seemingly abandoned V-twins, turning to the single-cylinder four-strokes for which the company is most famous, notably the Bullet. Before World War I, Britain had been the world's economic superpower. With rapid growth and a vast empire, the country benefited from significant wealth and resources, but still wasn't ready for the economic impact of the biggest conflict in history. When the war erupted in the summer of 1914, Britain faced market panic and an unprecedented financial crisis. Not only did the government need to reassure the markets, it had to prepare itself for the almost unimaginable economic demands of war on an industrial scale, a scale never seen before either in terms of monetary or human cost.

The government turned to direct taxes – on both property and income – on a far greater scale than ever before. In 1913, income tax was only paid by 2 per cent of the population, but during the war another 2.4 million people became liable so that, by 1918, four times as many people were paying income tax as before the war. How this money was spent – or used to repay loans – was therefore now decided by government rather than the people who earned it.

There was also massive borrowing from the public through the war bonds scheme, only repaid in 2014 when historically low interest rates meant that the fixed 3.5 per cent paid on war bonds finally looked high: the same rate had been paid

through the 1970s and early 1980s when inflation ran at over 20 per cent. The government had also cut itself free from the Gold Standard with the Currency and Bank Notes Act of 1914, the Bank of England thus being able to increase the amount of money available by simply printing it, even though this risked inflation and so rising prices.

So, although Britain was ultimately victorious, the effects of war would be felt for many years. Foreign trade, a key part of the British economy, had been badly damaged with countries cut off from the supply of British goods. This allowed countries not affected by the war to build up their own industries and become no longer reliant on Britain, competing directly instead. As a result, by 1920 Britain was experiencing the deepest recession in its history. The public was hit by higher taxes, the effective confiscation of savings when war bonds were not repaid, rising prices and the loss of jobs and earnings with the collapse of exports. It was into this world that Royal Enfield, like many others, had to sell its products. Big V-twins were luxuries few could justify, even if they could afford one.

THE COST OF RIDING

The main costs associated with owning a motorcycle were very much down to the purchase price and fuel economy. The Finance Act 1920 added a 'Duty on licences for mechanically propelled vehicles', which was to be hypothecated – that is, the revenue would be exclusively dedicated to a particular expenditure, namely the newly established Road Fund. Excise duties specifically for mechanically propelled vehicles were first imposed in 1921, along with the requirement to display a vehicle licence (tax disc). Third-party insurance would not become compulsory until introduced with the Road Traffic Act 1930 and compulsory testing not introduced until 1936; even then, passing the driving test allowed the licence holder to drive most things, even if he (and it usually was a he) had simply been observed riding a motorcycle around a city square. Learners on a so-called provisional (but easily renewed) licence would not be limited to 250cc until 1961. Until then, the only reason to own a small capacity motorcycle was purchase price, perhaps combined with a need for good fuel economy. A low horsepower rating also helped to keep taxes low.

Royal Enfield's response was to focus on a new range of single-cylinder motorcycles, and understandably so. But there was one last hurrah for the V-twins and, as we have discovered, the company's current CEO's all-time favourite Royal Enfield.

SPECIAL K

Throughout the 1920s and 1930s the firm manufactured a range of bewildering and fast-changing variety, at the pinnacle of which was the Model K, a large capacity V-twin intended primarily for sidecar use. JAP-powered V-twins had been a feature of the range since 1912, but from 1925 Royal Enfield's own engine was used. Displacing 976cc at first, this side-valve unit was stretched to 1140cc for export models only from January 1933. The 976cc K went on sale in 1933, with the 1140cc KX model making its first appearance in 1936. Sales at home were delayed until 1938.

'The last word in luxury motorcycling' was how Royal Enfield headlined the Model K in its 1938 sales brochure. It was now also powered by the mighty 1140cc, side-valve, twin-cylinder engine with totally enclosed valve gear and Royal Enfield's dry-sump lubrication system. This powerful unit combined with a heavyweight, four-speed, hand-controlled gearbox to ensure that the Model K with standard ratios was ideal for both sidecar and solo use. Lucas 6V Magdyno lighting was standard, as was black enamel finish with gold lining. The top of the range Model KX featured detachable and interchangeable wheels and was marketed in solo form at £77/10s – about half the price of a Brough SS100. But in solo form the KX's boast of 80mph (129km/h) performance was very much put in the shade by George Brough's 100mph

(161km/h) guarantee. Remarkably, the KX was one of no fewer than eighteen different models marketed by Royal Enfield in the 1938 season.

If the original KX looked a bargain up against the Brough in period, today it's an absolute snip given that it's doubtful anyone riding a pre-war motorcycle is going to be challenging motorway speed limits; £20,000 to £30,000 should secure a fine example, although finding one might be a bigger challenge than raising the cash. They are rare, with only about 600 made: one owner estimates there are fewer than 200 left.

Mike Woodford's father and grandfather were both fans and he has inherited the enthusiasm for the big twins in more ways than one:

I purchased the bike from my mother when Dad passed away in 2013. It is a Royal Enfield Model K, with the 1140cc motor and first registered on 25 March 1937. My father acquired it on 17 February 1967. He already owned one that had belonged to his father – ADL 170, with the 976cc engine – and put an advert for spares in the Isle of Wight County Press and was delighted when the bike came with its consecutive alphanumeric registration: BDL 171. My father restored the bike over a forty-year period, in-between working and married life with three children. This and one other RE 1140 are the only two of this type to have been registered on the Island, according to the RE archives. As well as buying the 1140cc Model K, I agreed to be custodian of the 976 and hopefully it will eventually pass on to a fourth generation Woodford.

It is meant to be a sidecar hauler and with its substantially heavier frame over the 976cc models it is quite a challenge to lift on to its rear centre stand. But riding it is wonderful once you have mastered the [four-speed] hand gear change. I imagine I am travelling in a two-wheeled Bentley, with the smoothness of the torquey low revving engine and comforting whine of the gearbox. It's not slow either: with the right gearing it can reach over 80mph. Just as well the large brakes are excellent too.

Despite Mike's rightful praise, production of the Royal Enfield KX stopped at the start of World War II, when the company switched to military contracts only, manufacturing 350cc models. However, one last KX was built, which was presented to military personnel. This final Royal Enfield KX was modified with styling more suited for the military and the sidecar's wheels were driven. This was, however,

Mike Woodford's family special Ks as detailed in the text.

The owner considers the big Enfield the equivalent of a two-wheeled Bentley. MIKE WOODFORD

the time when the military's focus was shifting to the then-new Jeep cars. The era of big cross-country motorcycles was coming to an end, although the singles would burnish Royal Enfield's off-roading credentials to a golden hue. As the V-twins went quietly into the night, the singles were about to shine brightly.

3

SINGLES BETWEEN THE WARS

As Royal Enfield's managing director Bob Smith had insisted, the company's post-war future would 'be met by producing existing models for the immediate future so that there will be the least possible delay in delivery'. So for 1919 Royal Enfield offered just two models at opposite ends of the motorcycling spectrum: the V-twin sidecar tugs from the previous chapter and the 225cc 2¼HP two-stroke lightweight first shown on the eve of war. Periodically revised and updated, the latter would remain a fixture of the Royal Enfield range up to World War II. Actually, the diminutive stroker had been presented

to the public in 1914 as a Ladies' bike, but due to the war few machines were made before 1919. The machine's frame is remarkable in that the top rail drops from the headstock to the bottom of the saddle tube, with a fuel tank carried well forward: not great for road holding, but allowing it to be ridden wearing a long skirt. Women were in fact early adopters in the UK of motorcycling as a sport and the layout was also commonplace in Italy to allow clerics to ride in their cassocks.

The well-made lightweight had a bore and stroke 64 × 70mm and was an excellent seller. It started a tradition,

2·25 h.p. Open-frame Model 201a
(Tax 30/-)
Similar in general specification to Model 201, but designed and built for the lady or gentleman who prefers not to wear special clothing when motor cycling. It has a unique frame with circular tank. A dressguard extends rearwards from the tank to protect the rider's clothes.

Price - £34 0 0 net cash
or £9 8 9 down, and twelve monthly instalments of
£2 11 0, including Insurance.

The open-frame Model 201a, ideal for riders in a skirt, apparently.

Although mainly finished in black enamel, the fuel tank showed a splash of Royal Enfield's traditional green paint. BONHAMS

with a 225cc two-stroke remaining in the Royal Enfield line-up until the closure of the Redditch factory in 1967. It was joined by the more conventional looking 'flat tank' Model 201 for the 1922 model year and was continuously updated and offered with upgraded specifications. Even a sportier version arrived with TT dropped handlebars and sports exhaust.

The power from the engine was originally sent to the back wheel through Enfield's own two-speed transmission. In the early models this was effected by a typical 'tram handle' gear-change lever up by the rider's hand, but the 1924 models were updated with such refinements as a kick-starter (rather than pushing) and foot-operated gear shift.

Also new in the 1924 catalogue was an updated open frame Model 201A, introduced in the catalogue as 'suitable for the lady or gentleman who wishes to use a motorcycle for shopping, riding to golf etc.' rather than simply the Ladies' model. The little 225cc achieved a number of racing successes: a gold medal in the ACU Six Days' Trial; five first places in the Worcester Motorcycle Club Hill Climb; and a win in a 100-mile (161km) rough track during the Rand Motorcycle Club's Open Lightweight Trial in South Africa. By 1928, the 200 range were all produced with saddle

tanks, starting with the two-speed 201 (also available in sports trim as the 200) and the three-speed 202, again available in a no-cost sports option as the 203. All could be specified with Maglita electric lights at extra cost.

THE FOUR-STROKE SINGLES ARRIVE

The year 1923 was a big one for Royal Enfield. Legendary designer Ted Pardoe joined the company and would go on to design many new models including the even more legendary Bullet. Pardoe was yet another trials fan with a reputation as a thinker and forward planner rather than a dirt under the fingernails type. His energy and drive would be a key part in Enfield's success and in 1925 he became Head of Development. But more immediately in 1923, after more than a decade of V-twins and almost a decade of two-strokes, it became clear that a more powerful and modern single-cylinder engine was needed to flesh out the range. Given Royal Enfield's hard-won reputation for quality, the decision to use the best power plant available, a JAP 350cc engine, came as no surprise.

The result was a total of eight models shown at London's Olympia Motorcycle Show, including two new motorcycles with JAP 350cc four-stroke singles, one side valve – the Model 350 – and a sports overhead valve option, the Model 351. From this moment on, a 350 single would remain in the Royal Enfield line until the present day. Shown alongside the brace of 350s and the four 225cc two-stroke models were two versions of the Woolsey V-twin powered sidecar outfit, with (Model 110) and without (Model 180) electrical equipment and lighting. All machines were fitted with foot gear changes and Enfield two-speed transmission, but in 1924 three-speeds were offered, initially on the four-strokes. At the same time in came internal expanding drum brakes and some machines had the new 346cc side-valve Enfield engine in preference to the JAP.

In 1925, Royal Enfield announced that the JAP engines would give way to the four-stroke singles of Ted Pardoe's in-house design, which would also see the three-speed Sturmey Archer gearbox standardized. Initially, there was a 346cc sports model with an ohv engine and features including an aluminium piston, 5in (127mm) drum brakes and close-ratio gearbox. Finding a ready market, Royal Enfield continued to expand the range and in 1926 a 488cc side-valve model followed, although it would be 1929 before this was offered with overhead valves and a twin-port head.

Another legendary Enfield figure, Tony Wilson-Jones, arrived at Royal Enfield in 1925. He would stay until the very end in 1970. Wilson-Jones would be responsible for setting up the company's apprentice training scheme, recruiting forty youngsters each year at fourteen years of age, fresh out of school, to be trained. This was a great way of ensuring that the company had skilled labour and would play a crucial role in the company's development, including expansion into India. Wilson-Jones had studied engineering at the City & Guilds College in London and was apprenticed with Daimler in Coventry and with Jack Sangster at BSA in Birmingham. He would become Head of Development at Royal Enfield, but one of his first tasks was to prepare the Isle of Man TT machines.

Wilson-Jones had four riders ready for the Junior (350cc) TT race on 15 June, riding twin-port ohv JAP-engined models. They were South African Charlie Young, George Reynard and two Irishmen, Stanley Woods and Gordon Burney. They did not do well: the best result was Young in seventh, with a disappointing DNF for Woods, given that he would become a TT legend.

More promising was a Royal Enfield trade delivery outfit taking part in the ACU Six Days' Trial for Commercial Sidecars, completing the demanding course without losing points and receiving a special certificate of merit. There were many other sporting successes throughout the year, including the Junior Ulster Grand Prix, Gordon Burney on a 344cc Royal Enfield winning the race at an average speed of

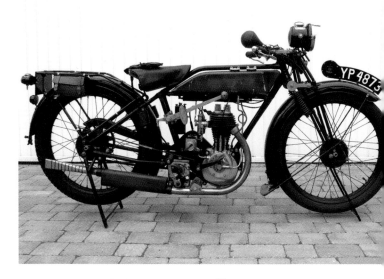

This 1927 Royal Enfield 2¾HP Standard Model was sold new via the Reading Motor Exchange, only resold in 1991 by its first owner, George Henry Keal. BONHAMS

An unrestored 1926 Royal Enfield 2¾HP Standard Model. BONHAMS

65.60mph (105.57km/h). W.F. (Fred) Bicknell was awarded the Presidents' Trials Cup and a gold medal in the Redditch Motorcycle Club half-day sporting trial on 24 October. A week later, J.E. Kettle on a similar machine won the Walker Cup in Dublin. In the Colmore Cup Trial, Bicknell gained a gold medal and J. Element and E.H. Clifton on an 8HP Royal Enfield sidecar won the silver medal. In the Victory Cup, both Bicknell and Element were awarded gold medals.

Enfield's sporting achievements continued from the off in 1926, when on 1 and 2 January Charlie Young won both the 350 and 600 solo events aboard a Royal Enfield 350 at the South African TT races along 200 miles (322km) of hilly roads in what is now the Kragga Kamma Game Park.

The cover of the 1928 Royal Enfield catalogue.

Back in Redditch, Tony Wilson-Jones was developing Pardoe's new single, which included touring one with a side-car around the Lake District during his honeymoon. He had also started preparing early for the Isle of Man TT race, which proved prescient, since the UK was hit by the 1926 General Strike that was called on 3 May and lasted until 12 May. But the 1926 TT is arguably when the Isle of Man's greatest challenge started on the road that would make it the most important race in the world for the next forty years. With the manufacturers still unhappy about the image of sidecar racing, the ACU scrapped the three-wheelers for 1926, together with the Ultra-Lightweight class, which suffered from a lack of entries. Thus the long-running format of Senior, Junior and Lightweight (500, 350 and 250cc) races was established, all three events being run over a distance of seven laps totalling 264.11 miles (425.04km).

The course had been improved considerably, with even the Mountain section tarmacked. Another change was a ban on methanol, forcing competitors to use ordinary petrol. With the fame of the TT spreading throughout Europe, while enhancing the reputation of the British factories, the Italians especially decided it was time they had a share of the glory, thus drawing entries from Garelli, Bianchi and Moto Guzzi.

Nevertheless, it was a British Cotton that won the opening Lightweight race, which almost produced an international incident when Italian Pietro Ghersi finished second on his Moto Guzzi, only to be excluded for using a different plug from the one specified on his entry form. It was cruel luck for Ghersi, who had led the opening six laps and looked a likely winner. On the final lap he had had to refuel, which enabled Paddy Johnston to win by just twenty seconds on his Cotton. The Italian's only consolation was a new lap record of 63.12mph (101.58km/h).

Velocette produced a new Junior contender for Alec Bennett. The 350cc ohc machine proved an instant winner, providing the popular Bennett with a record-breaking third TT win and new lap and race records. The Senior produced the first-ever 70mph (113km/h) lap – set by Simpson on his AJS – and a victory for Stanley Woods on his Norton debut.

Clearly these were races won by names that would go on to become part of TT and racing folklore, yet Royal Enfield was far from disgraced. The factory's riders were Gordon Burney, George Reynard, Charlie Young and Cecil Barrow, with Bicknell, more of a trials rider as well as a works foreman, joining the team as reserve. When Barrow fell and broke his collarbone in practice, Bicknell inherited his rides, starting with the Lightweight and taking fifth at 48.47mph (78km/h), the only Enfield rider to finish. In the Junior Race, Burney took sixth place, with Bicknell the only other Enfield rider to finish, albeit back in twenty-sixth place. Enfield did not contest the Senior.

Just a week after the TT, on 27 June, Bicknell was back competing in more familiar territory during the Scottish Six Days' Trial. He and T.H. Garner rode machines with the newly designed 346cc ohv engines with inclined (rather than parallel) valves and duplex springs, plus enclosed rocker gears and pushrods. Garner failed to finish, but Bicknell was awarded a silver medal.

On 17 July Reynard won the 50-mile (80km) Handicap Race during the Open Speed Trials in Saltburn-by-the-Sea in North Yorkshire. T. Stewart came second in the 350cc class of the 1926 Ulster Grand Prix at 64.22mph (103.35 km/h). During the ISDT, that year in the Peak District in

Derbyshire, the works team comprised Garner, Bicknell and Mrs P.C. Spokes on 350cc machines and C. Patrick with a 976cc V-twin outfit. Garner was forced to retire and Mrs Spokes lost too many points to be classified, but Bicknell and Patrick won gold awards.

Cecil Barrow, recovered from his Isle of Man fall, took part in the 1926 Hutchinson Hundred at Brooklands, a 100-mile (161km) handicap event for all types of machines up to 1000cc. He rode his Isle of Man Royal Enfield Lightweight TT entry, a 250 JAP-powered single now running on alcohol, with Brooklands fishtail exhausts. He won, receiving the Mellano Cup for his efforts. A month later at the Ulster Grand Prix, Royal Enfield's T. Stewart finished second at 64.02mph (103.03km/h). The company was able to underpin this competition success with a solid economic position in spite of a strike in May, and an expansion of the Hewell Road plant took place towards the end of the year.

A 1928 350 Sport with ohv motor, but still with a hand gear change. BONHAMS

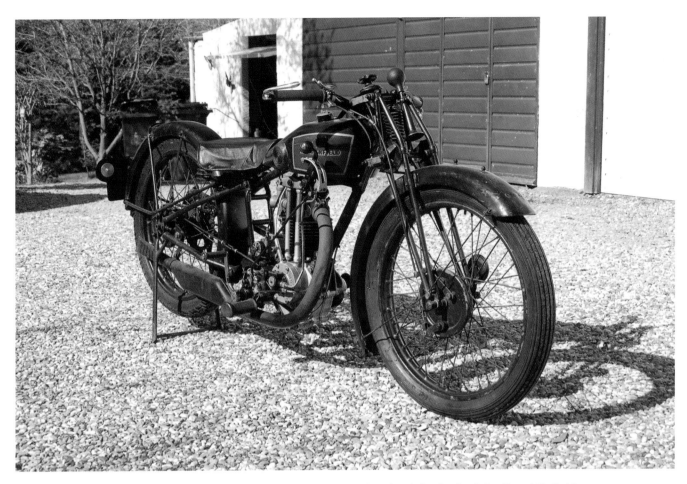

It is remarkable how the switch from 'flat' to saddle tanks modernized the look of the Royal Enfield range. BONHAMS

OFF-ROAD SUCCESS

Given that most of the hierarchy at Royal Enfield were fans of off-road sport, it is a measure of the importance of the TT that the factory continued to chase success on the Isle of Man. At least the 1927 TT only brought one DNF from eight entries and a best result of fourth place for Reynard in the Junior. At last in 1928 there was success of a sort, when Barrow finished second in the Lightweight TT. Even so, he was a good way behind winner Frank Longman on an OK-Supreme and only just ahead of Edwin Twemlow's DOT. Gradually, Royal Enfield's efforts at the TT would drift away in a sea of DNFs and a realization that the Isle of Man was not really part of the factory's DNA.

In the meantime, L.A. Welch and Bicknell won gold medals in the Cotswold Cup Trial in February, Welch also being

awarded a gold medal in the Victory Cup Trial in Birmingham, with four other Enfield riders receiving bronze medals. In the Redditch 'Freak' Hill Climb at Morton Bank, a young Jack Booker won the amateur class on a Royal Enfield and would go on to become another well-known figure in the company in later years.

Royal Enfield was also doing well in racing events on the Continent, but it was to the ISDT again that the factory turned for its real success. For 1928, it was staged over the moors of Yorkshire, the Enfield team being Welch, Reynard and Betty Lermitte. All took home gold medals, with Lermitte finishing despite her exhaust parting company from her steed. In October, Lermitte would go on to win the Stanley Bernard Challenge Cup aboard her ISDT machine.

The road range was also on a roll, adopting saddle tanks for a far more modern look and centre-spring (rather than side-spring, Druid style) forks. Most now had three speeds and some models were even offered with four. But if the number of models offered in 1928 appeared excessive, the 1929 range (for delivery in 1930) went over the top: the Royal Enfield catalogue boasted a range of fourteen machines, the most the factory would ever offer. Among the new offerings, and a new set of model numbers, was a twin-port ohv 488cc already mentioned, Pardoe's upgrade of his side-valve single, alongside a 350 version. All four 225cc machines from 1928 remained unchanged, except for a reduction in price. The V-Twin acquired a Sturmey-Archer three-speed box.

However, shaky stock-market trading, as investors started to worry that the spending and boom of the Roaring Twenties had been overdone, reached breaking point on 24 October – 'Black Thursday' – and the Dow Jones Industrial Average in New York lost over 10 per cent on top of a similar plunge the day before. Within two years it would lose 90 per cent of its value. Royal Enfield was one of the fortunate that survived the Depression, but the glories in racing and the variety of machines on offer would never be matched again as the economic hardships that held sway for much of that decade started to bite. Yet as people abandoned cars for motorcycles or even bicycles, Royal Enfield was able to survive with nimble management. In addition, and contrary to common belief, the 1930s economic plight affected very specific groups and many people – perhaps even most in some parts of the country – enjoyed a good and improving standard of living that made the coming war seem unthinkable.

A nicely restored 1928 Royal Enfield 3½HP Model 501. BONHAMS

The side-valve layout of the 488cc single is obvious from this aspect. BONHAMS

THE 1930 ROYAL ENFIELD RANGE ANNOUNCED IN 1929

The first J model was listed for 1930 and throughout the decade there would be a large number of models, from small two-strokes to bigger side-valve four-strokes, literally catalogued from A to Z. These included those listed below for 1930, as well as the Model J2 488cc twin-port ohv single and the side-valve V-twins, the Model K (976cc) and occasionally the L (570cc). Royal Enfield made much of their integral oil tank, hidden inside the engine cases, which negated the need for a separate oil tank that might split and oil lines that were prone to leaks. There were also mechanical oil pumps, even on the Model A, and valve gear was increasingly enclosed as Royal Enfield once again led the industry to modernity.

All models were available with lighting as an option identified by the suffix L, for example the Model KL. There was also a bewildering variety of sidecars, including a boxed-in one 'as used by the GPO'. But the really radical news would be the Model Z Cycar for 1932. Other models were:

* Model A: 225cc two-stroke vertical single
* Model B: 225cc side-valve vertical single
* Model C, F and G: 346cc side-valve single, with improving specification identified by later letters
* Model D, H and HA: 488cc side-valve single variants identified as above; the D had a vertical cylinder, the others a 'sloper'
* Model CO, E, J and JA: 488cc ohv single variants; the E had a vertical cylinder, the others a 'sloper'
* Model K: 976cc side-valve V-twins.

Throughout the 1930s Royal Enfield manufactured a range of bewildering and fast-changing variety. 'Slopers' with inclined engines were a feature of the decade's early years, one such new introduction for 1930 being this Model G, an ohv 350. BONHAMS

This particular machine is an example of the GL (De Luxe) model, which came with Lucas magdyno electrics as standard and is equipped with the optional four-speed gearbox. A relative rarity today, the Model G was renamed 'Bullet' for 1933 and continued in production until replaced by a new 'vertical' model for 1936. BONHAMS

A NEW DECADE

So, with such an ambitious expansion of the range, 1930 should have gone well for Royal Enfield, especially given the positive press coverage of those motorcycles' achievements. On 6 February, atop a frozen lake in Sweden, Edward Magner, the country's Royal Enfield importer, broke the world speed record with a sidecar combination. Later in the year Billy Pringle established a new Australian two-way flying start 350cc solo record for the quarter mile at 90.99mph (146.43km/h) on a 346cc Royal Enfield.

On the competition front, things also started well. In April, six Enfields took part in the Scottish Six Days' Trial: L.A. Welch on a 225cc solo; Campbell Spiers, Fred Bicknell and Betty Lermitte on 346cc solos; J.O. Stewart Junior on a 488cc solo; and G. Patrick with a 488cc sidecar combination. The first four finished the event, although Welch's little machine struggled and failed at one point, meaning settling for silver, which Betty Lermitte was also awarded. Spiers and Bicknell won a silver cup apiece.

The year's ISDT was reputed to be the toughest yet, taking place across Germany, Austria, Switzerland, Italy and France. Welch, this time armed with a 488cc ohv single, was one of the three members of the Great Britain team,

although he was beaten into second place in the UK's standings by H.S. Perrey on one of the dominant Ariels. Other Enfield riders included Bicknell, who had a dreadful event, breaking down (rescued with a tow from Betty Lermitte) and eventually abandoning the race, having lost his passport and becoming trapped in Italy. Lermitte at least finished and won a silver medal.

And that was about it for Royal Enfield's competition department, until World War II was done with at least. Welch was the sole rider of a Royal Enfield in the 1931 ISDT, held in north Italy, and only an occasional favoured privateer would race a Redditch-built motorcycle in the Isle of Man TT from now on. Cloth needed to be cut, and the Competition Department was where the scissors were biggest. But, as we shall see in Chapter 9, post-war there would once again be successes, especially off-road.

1931 RANGE UPDATES AND INTRODUCING THE BULLET

In 1931, all the four-stroke singles become 'slopers', with the cylinder inclined forward, albeit by much less than the 30 degrees or so adopted by trendsetters BSA. Inclining

From 1933, Royal Enfield's ohv singles became Bullets – 'Made like a gun, goes like a Bullet' being the slogan. Though Enfield's parts lists and catalogues can be confusing, it seems that the 'JF' Bullet was initially listed with an optional 4-valve cylinder head, in line with makers such as Rudge, but this was later discontinued in favour of the 2-valve option, the model being retitled the 'J2' in 1938. BONHAMS

This 499cc Bullet was registered in July 1937 and has the 'JF' engine prefix, but the 2-valve, twin-port cylinder head. BONHAMS

the cylinder forward brought a number of benefits: the exhaust valve, often the most fragile component in an engine, was better cooled; the new trend of placing 'saddle' fuel tanks above frame rails meant that, by moving the cylinder head forward, those frame rails could be lowered and so, in turn, could the saddle; and thus the centre of gravity was lowered, improving road holding. And the motorcycle-buying public loved the look, especially in twin-port form, which allowed an exhaust pipe on both sides of the motorcycle. Thus the Model J gained two ports and an overbore (to 80 × 99.25mm bore and stroke), growing displacement to 499cc, and more radically still there was a 4-valve option with the Model JF31. Similarly, the Model H31's bore and stroke grew to 85.5 × 99.25mm to give 570cc.

The following year came the announcement of the Bullet name, although in truth it was very different to the postwar version that remains so loved today. Instead, it was closely related to the slopers that predated it and Enfield's addition of a new Model B with 248cc (64 × 77mm bore and stroke available in side [Model B] and ohv [BO] versions). The new Bullets were first displayed in November 1932 at the Olympia Motorcycle Show in London, all with twin-port cylinder heads, four-speed gearboxes, aluminium primary-chain cases, high-level exhausts and high-compression pistons. The 500 had enclosed pushrod tubes from the off and these were adopted on the 250 and 350 Bullet for the 1934 model year.

Thus the Bullet designation really indicated the top of the range ohv sporting versions of Royal Enfield's evolving range, with power delivered at very high rpm by the single-cylinder standards of the era. The 1935 catalogue claims were 12bhp at 5,700rpm for the 246cc Bullet, the 346cc version giving 16bhp at 5,600 and the 488cc Bullet pushing out almost 25bhp at just 100 fewer rpm. By contrast, the 976cc V-twin was rated at just 22bhp at 3,400rpm.

THREE- AND 4-VALVE CYLINDER HEADS

However, the 1935 catalogue didn't mention something that was new but presumably, given its rarity, an option for favoured riders: a 3-valve cylinder head on the Model LO. As we have seen, the first 4-valve machine had entered the Royal Enfield range in 1931 with the Model JF. This bike had the near-square bore dimensions of 85 × 85.5mm that continued to be used until 1936 for the 500 bikes and was also used for the big V-twins. The 4-valve 500s were delivered with chrome tanks and instrumentation on a panel in the tank, upgraded for 1932 when the Model LF was introduced, having pushrod tunnels cast into the cylinder casting and either a three-speed hand change or a four-speed foot-change gearbox. High-compression pistons were among many factory tuning options, along with upswept exhaust pipes.

There was a frame redesign and further engine improvements in 1933. One of the major issues with the 4-valve engines was the cracking of cylinder heads between the exhaust ports when the machines were ridden hard and especially when raced. Bronze heads were used on racing machines to reduce the chance of the cracking that was commonplace on the cast-iron heads.

The high-compression pistons were sold with an expectation that pure benzole (an alcohol-based fuel) would be used and the maximum power was a claimed 29.5bhp. The standard 4-valve machine claimed 24.5bhp.

The final year that Royal Enfield offered factory support to a TT rider was 1935, providing a Model LF for Cecil Barrows, who came eighth in the Senior event, beaten by Moto Guzzis, DKWs, Nortons and one HRD Vincent. But by now the LF had already been dropped from Royal Enfield's catalogue in favour of a 3-valve version intended to address the head-cracking issues of the earlier 4-valve machines. This was the Model LO with two inlet and one exhaust valve, all working in parallel rather than the pent-roof design of the 4-valve head, although more impressive to most was the fully enclosed valve gear. But the power of the LO proved significantly less than the LF and the model was quickly dropped in favour of a completely new 4-valve machine in 1936, reviving the JF designation, although most knew it simply as the Bullet.

As with the rest of the 1936 four-stroke single range the new Royal Enfield Model JF featured a vertical cylinder, a layout that remains to this day and was also adopted for the parallel twins. The head redesign did reduce cracking and bronze heads were still available as an option for buyers who intended their new motorcycle to be used in competition. But rather than being a purpose-built competition motorcycle this new Model JF was essentially the standard J fitted with a revised barrel, cylinder head and valve gear, as well as being delivered with a chrome tank, guards and a primary-chain case. The model was offered again in 1936 and 1937 but was dropped for 1938, although the 4-valve head remained available as an option for that year only, making it the final multi-valve model that Royal Enfield would sell until the new 650 twins arrived.

BIG CHANGES IN 1933

The year started with sadness, when founding partner and joint managing director, Bob Walker Smith, passed away. His association with Enfield lasted until his death on 6 February 1933 at the age of seventy-five. His son, the Major, who had been joint managing director with his father since 1914, assumed full control of the Enfield Cycle Company, the holding company of Royal Enfield. And the first thing he had to do was oversee the launch of a radical new Royal Enfield, the Cycar.

The 148cc Cycar was a reaction to tax changes by a government desperate to raise cash without damaging an already fragile economy. As we have seen initially, vehicle taxation was hypothecated – that is, reserved exclusively for spending to the benefit of those who paid it, in this instance the Road Fund. But government was finding that expansion of the road network was costing far more than vehicle taxation raised. In a minute to his officials in November 1925, the then Chancellor Winston Churchill wrote that:

> Entertainments may be taxed; public houses may be taxed; racehorses may be taxed... and the yield devoted to the general revenue. But motorists are to be privileged for all time to have the whole yield of the tax on motors devoted to roads. Obviously this is all nonsense ... Such contentions are absurd, and constitute ... an outrage upon the sovereignty of Parliament and upon common sense.

Publicity photograph for the radical Cycar.
ROYAL ENFIELD

The brochure for the Cycar was as unusual as the bike.

A 'raid on the Road Fund' was feared by motoring organizations, but they could do little to stop it despite support in Parliament. In 1927, Churchill made the first of his two 'raids' on the Road Fund, the beginning of its end. The whole of the Road Fund's £12m was absorbed into government coffers by 1937, although it limped on, in name only, until the 1950s.

There was justification for this. The 1930 Royal Commission on Transport reported that two-thirds of the maintenance cost of roads – despite the existence of the Road Fund – was met by general and local taxation. The nail in the coffin was the Salter Report of 1932, which recognized that motorized road vehicles were guilty of 'using the common highway for private profit, while endangering public safety, amenity, and capital'.

So the UK's taxation of vehicles underwent considerable changes, as the government sought to balance the books. One of these was replacing the under-224lb reduced road tax category in 1932 with a new under-150cc tax classification. The 1930 Royal Enfield catalogue actually reassured would-be buyers that the increase of the 224lb class from 200lb was a given and that the lightweight 350 Model C31 would comply even with lighting: this meant annual taxation of just 30/- (£1.50), half the amount of the next category and far less than the £12 typically paid by a car owner. With the switch to a 150cc limit for the lowest tax rate, suddenly the entire Royal Enfield range, even the lowly 225cc strokers, was expensive to tax.

THE CYCAR, MODEL Z – FOLLOWED BY THE MODEL X

The new 148cc two-stroke was largely unremarkable, with a bore and stroke of 56 × 60mm, but, where most competitors used a bought-in Villiers motor, the design and manufacture was all done in house. Unlike its 225cc predecessor, the cylinder was inclined forward, a feature the Model A quickly adopted, although the Cycar motor retained the external flywheel. However, like the Model A, the Cycar's had roller main bearings and the cylinder head was not detachable. The three-speed gearbox retained the older model's hand change. Not only was lighting standard, there was even a small battery for a parking light.

But most remarkable was the enclosed pressed-steel bodywork that was unlike anything else of the time. Post-war, the fashion for a fully enclosed look arguably started in scooter-mad Italy with the 1948 Moto Major 350, followed by the 1956 Aermacchi Chimera. Even Vincent got in on the act with the 1955 Black Knight, followed by the Ariel Arrow in 1958. On the filthy winter roads of Britain anything that made cleaning a motorcycle easier had some merit, but motorcyclists would have none of it, preferring style over weather protection. Eventually the fashion passed.

But for a humble commuter it made perfect sense, as likely to be bought out of necessity rather than to join in motorcycling's fine sport. Royal Enfield described the Cycar as 'an economical, reliable lightweight of unique design, which will take you anywhere and keep you clean'. The pressed-steel bodywork kept the oily motor and chain away from the rider, while the leg shields and generous mudguards protected him or her from road dirt.

The frame was a single steel pressing enclosing the motor, gearbox and external flywheel. Detachable leg shields completed the look. This was a stylish take on personal transport when lightweight motorcycles were, for many, a grim commuting necessity and Enfield's strapline of 'safe, clean, simple and economical' may well have been a selling point rather than the turn-off it might seem today. Only a few Cycars survive, oddly including a few in the United States, of the some 1,500 that were built between 1931 and 1936.

The follow-on was the far more conventional Model X, available from April 1933. A much more orthodox-looking machine, with a tubular frame, saddle tank and the engine in full view, it failed to find buyers and lasted just one year. This was despite the motor being considerably revised, with a twin-port vertical cylinder, and there are even tales of unsold stock being scrapped in preparation for the war

effort. It was replaced with the remarkably similar Model T, which featured an ohv motor of almost identical dimensions but with a four-speed gearbox and internal flywheel. Like its two-stroke forebear, the Model T was described as offering sporting performance with low running costs and managed to survive in the Royal Enfield catalogue until 1938, again outlived by the 225cc Model A. By now, the people at Redditch had realized that they were famous for the much-loved big singles, most especially the Bullet. But as the storm clouds of war gathered once more there was time for one more tiny two-stroke that would actually gain fame as the Flying Flea in World War II.

4

THE WAR YEARS

Cover of the 1940 Royal Enfield catalogue, ominously subtitled 'war time list'.

The wartime two-wheeler that Royal Enfield is most famous for is the WD-RE, the tiny troop transport everybody called the Flying Flea. Inspiration for the Flying Flea, a 125cc lightweight intended to parachute alongside British forces into enemy territory during World War II, ironically came from a German DKW design, via a Danish engineer.

In 1916, Jørgen Skafte Rasmussen founded a factory in Zschopau, Germany, to produce steam fittings. He tried building a steam-engined car, the *Dampf Kraft Wagen* ('steam-powered car'), which became the initials of his company. It failed to sell, but more conventional cars followed and were successful. Skafte then made a two-stroke toy engine in 1919, called *Des Knaben Wunsch* – DKW again, this time 'the boy's wish'. Pleased with his efforts, Skafte gave an evolution of this motor two wheels and turned to selling these modest vehicles – scooters and motorcycles – with a move into production in the early 1920s. This led to another change of name, if not initials: DKW became *Das Kleine Wunder* ('the little wonder'), purveyors of very modest – and not especially wonderful – two wheelers that were cheap, utterly conventional, but dependable two-stroke transport.

By the late 1920s, however, DKW had become a serious player, building more than 40,000 powered two wheelers in 1928 and becoming probably the biggest motorcycle manufacturer on earth. By 1938, a supercharged DKW was good enough to win the Junior TT with Ewald Kluge, the reason that Audi's sports car is called the TT: DKW was one of the four manufacturers subsumed into the Auto Union that begat Audi and perhaps the most tenuous claim to fame ever made by a car manufacturer. But later Deeks (as Brits tend to call them) had the four circles of the Auto Union – and still used by Audi – on its badging, so the link is undeniable.

In 1929, a German engineer, Adolf Schnürle, developed the two-stroke's loop-scavenging system. With two intake ports, one on each side of the exhaust port, angled so that incoming fuel would flow to fill the entire combustion chamber, it would also push the charge from the previous combustion cycle into the exhaust port. This avoided the need for heavy deflector pistons and made the motor less prone to overheating, more powerful and reduced fuel consumption. No wonder it was part of the new DKW RT125's architecture and that the RT125 (*Reichs Typ*, or National Model) was quick (a very relative term), reliable and cheap to buy and run. This was the bike that would be taken as post-war reparations and become the prototype for the BSA Bantam, Harley-Davidson Hummer and the first Yamaha motorcycle, the YA-1 Red Dragonfly.

But pre-war the original design displaced just 98cc and was listed as the DKW RT98, with a tweaked version known as the RT1003PS (3PS being circa 3bhp). And then, in early 1938, the Nazi-controlled German government instructed DKW to revoke its contract with the Dutch importers, R.S. Stokvis en Zonen of Rotterdam, when the Dutch company refused to banish its Jewish owners. But in the Netherlands

the DKW RT100 was a very popular lightweight model due to lower tax rates for motorcycles weighing less than 132lb (60kg).

So, rather than capitulate to the Nazis, Stokvis sought a factory that could manufacture sufficient numbers of a near-identical replacement for the diminutive Deek in double-quick time. This led to delivery of an example of the DKW RT100 to Royal Enfield. Chief designer, Ted Pardoe, became responsible for the faithful reproduction of the RT, aided and abetted by Stokvis engineers with experience of tuning the 98cc DKW motor for racing, taking the opportunity to stretch the bore and stroke from the DKW's 50 × 50mm to grow the motor to a full 125cc.

A ROYAL BABY

Two prototype versions of this new 'Royal Enfield' RE125 were displayed in Rotterdam in April 1939 to be marketed by Stokvis as the Royal Baby. A Dutch newspaper dated 25 April 1939 reported that:

> During manufacturing, the experience gained by the Stokvis company with those small motorcycles was amply utilized. For example, whenever there had been difficulties with certain DKW parts they were redesigned and replaced. There have also been searched-for improved materials for all parts, so that weight savings are achieved, so that the definite product of

1950 DKW RT125W.

Major Smith presents the 'Royal Baby' at the Redditch offices. ROYAL ENFIELD

'the Royal Baby' weighs only 48.8kg [108lb]. Fully equipped, a motorcycle must weigh less than 60kg [to qualify for the lowest taxation class], so that the Royal Baby, including petrol, oil, mirror, horn, pillion, remains below that weight limit. The material used for the Royal Baby meets the highest demands.

The engine is a two-stroke unit engine of 124.8cc cylinder capacity, bore and stroke 53.8 × 55mm. A so-called Typhoon fuel flush has been applied, so that the engine does not 'four-stroke'. Lubrication is achieved by oil mixing through the petrol. A flywheel magnet of completely new design has been used. The flywheel does not have to be disassembled for checking points or cleaning. A special silencer is fitted, which effectively dampens the sound. The Royal Baby has a completely welded tubular frame with pressed-steel fork. The gearbox is in unit with the crankcase which has a drive gear on ball bearings, the other shafts on silent bronze bushes. There are three gears with manual gear shift, freewheel and kick-starter. Furthermore, the machine has internally expanding

drum brakes and Dunlop 2.50 × 19in tyres. Undoubtedly, the Royal Baby is an interesting machine with clever technical details and a neat appearance.

Royal Enfield talked of an initial delivery of 100 machines, pencilled in for the first week of May, with the initial swollen order book promised to be fulfilled during June. But only a handful were made and even fewer actually delivered to the Netherlands. As the clouds of war gathered once more Royal Enfield and its compatriots were far more prepared than they had been in 1914. This started amongst the visitors to the 1935 Leipzig fair, which included two executives from BSA, the senior being James Leek. Upon his return to Small Heath, Leek warned the directors that war was inevitable and, despite the lack of government backing since 1918, the board courageously sanctioned Leek's request for extra cash to allow BSA to resume its role as a private arms manufacturer. When war was declared, BSA's planning office and tool room had been on overtime for three years. Down the road, Royal Enfield was similarly ready to contribute all it could: after all, the managing director had risen to become a Major in the previous conflict and would have been party to Leek's warning that he had seen 'the bullets [that] were for England' being made in Germany.

BSA was not alone in preparing for rearmament. From 1935, the British government had started the 'shadow' factory scheme, which hints at secrecy but was nothing of the sort. The Luftwaffe's General Erhard Milch was paid a consultancy fee for advice on shadow factories in Birmingham and Coventry in late 1937. 'Back-up' factories might have been a better term, with the new facilities intended to offer an alternative to the main factories should they have to cease production following attack. Naturally they were camouflaged as soon as war was declared.

This period running up to World War II is often portrayed as one of naive appeasement just waiting for Winston Churchill to grasp the levers of power and belatedly prepare Britain for the conflict to come. But in truth Prime Minister Stanley Baldwin had been trying to rearm the country and believed that this cost him the 1937 general election. In the Peace Ballot of 1935 over ten million British voters petitioned for disarmament versus fewer than 900,000 opposing the idea. People wanted any available money to be spent on the aftermath of the Depression and most believed that Britain could sit out the Nazi's takeover of continental Europe, Switzerland style. This was the real naivety that tied the hands of politicians such as Baldwin, even though Hitler was already demanding designs for bombers that could reach Washington from Europe, with Britain earmarked as George Orwell's Airstrip One, or at least feared as a base that could disrupt missions from France. Fortunately, people such as Leek saw the inevitable and, along with many others, prepared for war through gritted teeth.

Finally, on 1 September 1939, Germany invaded Poland after having feigned a number of border incidents to test the Allies' mettle. The United Kingdom responded with an ultimatum to Germany to cease military operations, but, on 3 September, with the ultimatum ignored, France and Britain, along with their empires, declared war on Germany. And that should have been the end of the Royal Baby.

MODEL WD-RE AKA THE FLYING FLEA

In 1940, Churchill authorized the formation of a Special Air Service Battalion, which became the Airborne Division under General Browning in 1941. The parachute regiment was formed in 1942, with transport after dropping

being BSA's 'Second Pattern Airborne' folding bicycle. The need for motorized transport was first recognized with the Welbike folding scooter, a 98cc two-stroke built by Excelsior at the direction of Station IX – the Inter Services Research Bureau – for use by Special Operations Executive (SOE). It still has the distinction of being the smallest motorcycle ever used by the British armed forces, but because of the small wheels it especially struggled in rough terrain.

So there followed a test of alternatives. The DKW RT100 motorcycle was tested first, as it was the lightest ready-made motorcycle. Able to climb out of steep ditches with some deft footwork, easily able to carry a passenger and light enough to be lifted over a fence, it was a good start – but not available. SOE then tested the derivative from Royal Enfield, essentially a revisited Royal Baby, resulting in the ordering of a prototype and an additional eighteen bikes in 1942. The evaluation was so successful that it was followed by an order for 4,000 of the 125cc machines, designated WD-REs (War Department Royal Enfields) for delivery in November 1943. By the end of the war, nearly 7,000 of the WD-REs had been dispatched to the armed forces.

War Department catalogue photograph of the WD-RE, aka the Flying Flea.

When Royal Enfield produced a limited-edition Bullet to remember the Flying Flea and the airborne troops who used it, the company went to considerable lengths to remind all of its history. ROYAL ENFIELD

The Flying Flea in its parachute cage, part of a small museum at Royal Enfield's Garage Café in Goa.

Officially known as the Airborne 125, it was first nick-named the Flying Flea by the British Army Red Berets parachute regiment when it was released for service duty in 1943. The name fitted perfectly, reflecting its light 130lb (59kg) weight and diminutive build, at just 26in wide × 75in long (660 × 1,905mm).

Of course, you can't just throw a motorcycle out of an aircraft and expect it to be more than scrap when found. So the Flying Flea came with handlebars stowed sideways and packed into a steel tubular frame called the 'Bird Cage', complete with its own parachute, ready to be dropped alongside troops. The Flying Flea proved its worth in Operation *Market Garden* when, in September 1944, the Allied forces launched the largest airborne operation ever, aiming to liberate parts of Holland and to capture key bridges that would give a route into the heart of Germany's industrial region.

Although ultimately unsuccessful, the operation gave the Flying Flea a chance to shine. At the Battle of Arnhem, Britain's 1st Airborne Division held out against German tanks for seven days, using Flying Fleas as messenger bikes. They were also shipped to France during the D-Day invasion. So good was the idea that over 4,000 Flying Fleas had been built by 1945.

BULLETS FOR THE WAR EFFORT

Royal Enfield's other two-wheeled contribution to the war effort was the four-stroke singles, some with family ties to the Bullet, although the name would be rested until 1948. Even so, Redditch seemed to turn out far more variety than the mighty BSA, despite making a fraction of the Small Heath factory's huge number of motorcycles, almost all of them M20s. The Royal Enfields produced for the military were: the WD/C 350 side valve; the WD/CO and G 350 ohv; the WD/D 250 side valve; and the WD/L 570cc SV. More than 29,000 of the military WD/C and WD/CO ohv models were supplied to Allied forces during World War II, some 2,800 going to the RAF. However, this was a tiny amount in comparison to the 126,334 motorcycles that BSA built during World War II, most of them the M20. Arguably less able than the competition, in truth the M20's big advantage was almost certainly that it was available. During the initial tests it had been in competition with machines from Matchless, Norton, Triumph and Royal Enfield and was considered the least able of the group. But BSA had been gearing up for war as early as 1935, well before the government had asked them to. So, while the military preferred the Matchless G3L

Royal Enfield WD training for dispatch rider service in 1941. A HERL INC

Circa 1944 346cc Model CO. In 1940, the WD (War Department) military Model C commenced delivery to UK armed forces and approximately 17,600 had been produced before the model was superseded by the ohv WD/CO in 1942. By the war's end, more than 29,000 WD/C and WD/CO models had been supplied to Allied forces, some 2,800 or so going to the RAF. BONHAMS

This late example of a Model CO carries two 'Établissement Général du Matériel du Mans' plaques, indicating that it was used by the French armed forces and was rebuilt in July 1950. BONHAMS

single and a side-valve twin from Triumph, Matchless – like Royal Enfield – could not promise the number of machines required and Triumph's drawings, prototypes and tooling had been destroyed in a bombing raid. BSA alone was tooled up and ready to build the numbers that the military needed. So the WM20, an otherwise unremarkable 350 side-valve single, would become the longest serving and most numerous motorcycle in British military history.

MOVING AWAY FROM MOTORCYCLES – AND GOING UNDERGROUND

The Enfield Cycle Company was also called upon to manufacture a variety of special equipment, so it was not just motorcycles during the war years. The company had to move markedly outside of its comfort zone as a respected motorcycle manufacturer, forming a number of war-work subsidiaries. Amongst them was Enfield Industrial Engines,

which built small, boxer (opposed twin-cylinder) diesels, and later marine engines. The liquid-cooled diesel engines were popular for generators and an air-cooled diesel followed, apparently one of the first in the world. The division that carried out these projects was listed as Enfield Industrial Engines and would resurface as an independent business when Enfield Cycles was bought up in the 1960s.

In June 1941, it was this part of Royal Enfield that moved from Redditch to old underground stone workings at Westwood Quarry, close to the ancient Wiltshire town of Bradford-on-Avon (a broad ford across the Avon, a few miles downstream from Bath). The old tunnels here were the legacy of the honey-coloured stone made most famous by nearby Bath; the stone is unusual in being mined rather than taken from an open quarry. Once commercially exhausted, the mine cum quarry was put to use for mushroom culture and later for secure storage, as it is today. Below quarrymen's homes, Upper Westwood is accessed via a long tunnel, its stone, flecked with rusty patches, still occasionally extracted when a match to an old building is needed.

1942

1895

1945

THESE PHOTOGRAPHS ILLUSTRATE THE TRANS-FORMATION OF THE ENTRANCE OF THE ANCIENT BATH STONE QUARRY OF 1895 TO THE MODERN UNDERGROUND FACTORY OF 1945. ONE OF THE MEN APPEARS IN THE PHOTOGRAPHS OF 1895 AND 1945.

Pages from a brochure that Royal Enfield produced at the end of World War II to explain the history of its Bradford-on-Avon factory. A HERL INC

The low ceilings of the mine are obvious.
A HERL INC

WELDING.

WELDING.

INSPECTION

CAPSTAN LATHE.

Motorcycle engines are visible in the upper image.
A HERL INC

However, during World War II it was a Royal Enfield factory for making guns and gunsights, as well as storage for the treasures of the British Museum and the Victoria and Albert Museum. Shifting production here made the factory less vulnerable to German bombers than Enfield's original home, avoiding being destroyed by a bombing raid of the sort that had razed Coventry the previous year. Nearby Birmingham suffered even more than Coventry, although the government used a D notice to prevent this being reported. A Nazi air raid on a BSA Small Heath factory resulted in the biggest single loss of life in a British factory during the war, with fifty-three killed and eighty-nine injured. Many were women, or those too young or too old to fight. It was six weeks before the final body was recovered. Yet nothing was reported beyond 'bombs fell on a West Midlands' town', because the government prohibited it and would continue to do so for thirty years. Birmingham was too important a manufacturing centre to let anybody know that it had been critically wounded. So, while the story of Coventry's horror is well known, Birmingham's is not, despite it receiving twice the tonnage of Nazi bombs as its near neighbour and 1,000 more fatalities. Indeed, only London was bombed more. Little wonder that Royal Enfield wanted to move south to the comparative safety of Bradford-on-Avon.

Ironically, Bradford-on-Avon became just as likely a site for German bombs when Joseph Goebbels ordered the Luftwaffe to divert their blitzes to English cities featured in a famous German tourist guide, the *Baedeker*. By following the River Thames, the Kennet and Avon Canal and finally the River Avon, Nazi bombers could find Bath and Bristol comparatively easily, even at night. Anyone or anything along the route could therefore find themselves bombed by an aircraft needing to dump its load for an emergency early trip back to Germany.

In the safety of the old Bath stone mine, the firm carried out the manufacture of Type 3 predictor sights for anti-aircraft guns and control equipment for Bofors guns. The Royal Enfield staff magazine put the Bradford-on-Avon workers' new hostel on the cover, erected to house people who had been brought in to work at the subterranean factory. It included a tea bar and restaurant, with frequent entertainment to keep up morale. However, this hostel, along with the brick-built housing blocks – the 'Red Bungalows' – were demolished by Wiltshire County Council post-war to make way for new council houses.

A map of the surroundings of the Enfield Hostel inside the magazine included various 'beauty spots', each of them public houses. The clue was in their names, although many are now closed, including 'The Seven Stars' and 'New Bear' in Bradford-on-Avon itself, 'The Prince of Wales' in Turleigh and 'The Greyhound' in Freshford.

When the war ended in 1945, Royal Enfield used the Bradford-on-Avon workers' engineering expertise to assemble motorcycles, notably the Interceptor. The company made motorcycles initially from stocks of spare parts. There was also the repurposing of the Flying Flea as a civilian model. The 250c Crusader, Meteor and Meteor Minor models were made at Greenland Mills, Bradford, until 1963; the Interceptor was made at the former Wilkins Brewery in Newtown, Bradford, and at Westwood until 1970. But that's for a later chapter.

5

THE BRITISH BULLET

Enfield had used the Bullet name for a car in an early incarnation of the business, followed by a trio of motorcycles in 1932. These sporty offerings had, for the time, advanced single-cylinder motors of 250, 350 and 500cc with four-speed gearboxes, Royal Enfield's trademark oil tank within the crankcase, chilled iron valve guides and nitrided valve stems. The Model G, which appeared in 1935, was, however, the true origin of the post-war Bullet, with a vertical cylinder replacing the previous slopers, totally enclosed valve gear and gear-driven magneto. Its bore and stroke of 70 × 90mm, giving 346cc, survives to the present day. But even this was a very different motorcycle to the new Bullet, designated the G2, which, unlike its predecessor, was never available with a rigid frame.

The reason for this is that when Royal Enfield revived the Bullet name in 1948 for its new 350cc sports roadster and trials model, both were offered with an innovative swinging arm rear suspension. In itself, a swinging arm was not a new idea. ABC had considered the idea in 1919 and the 1934 Matchless Silver Hawk had a viable swinging-arm system. Vincent's pivoted rear fork was very similar and a paper by Australian Phil Irving – who had worked for Vincent – persuaded Royal Enfield engineer Tony Wilson-Jones that this was the future. Ironically, it would be Rex McCandless, a successful former motorcycle racer and designer from Northern Ireland, who would patent the idea in 1949, something Royal Enfield and Vincent presumably overlooked.

Rex McCandless had, during the war, worked in aviation, subsequently becoming a vehicle mechanic until, in 1943, going into business with his brother Cromie to repair vehicles for the Ministry of Supply. It was at this time that he built his own motorcycle, which became the prototype for the successful featherbed frame adopted by Norton. Harold Daniell gave the frame its name after his first test ride, saying that it was like 'riding on a featherbed' and so easy to ride fast because it could be more softly sprung than the 'garden gate' plunger frame – and the name stuck. The twin cradle loop that formed the mainframe and the swinging arm look unexceptional to us now, but that's because the layout became so widely adopted as to become ubiquitous, with the genius of McCandless – and Tony Wilson-Jones – hiding in plain sight.

An early (1951) Bullet, nicely presented. BONHAMS

A later (c.1957) Bullet in trials specification. BONHAMS

Tony Wilson-Jones was the man behind this G2 Bullet (and many other Enfields). He was a long-time factory development engineer and talented off-road rider, a trait of many of Royal Enfield's inner circle. With his expertise in both trial and engineering, Wilson-Jones knew exactly what he wanted from a competition motorcycle and how to achieve it. He was also able to persuade the conservative Royal Enfield management to green-light the two most significant features of the new 1948 Bullet. One was the factory's own two-way oil-damped (compression and rebound) telescopic fork, one of the most effective early designs. Tested off-road, it incorporated a breather system and gauze to filter displaced oil and offered what was then a remarkable 6in (152mm) of movement.

More controversial still, Wilson-Jones introduced Enfield's own brand of swinging-arm frame. That rear suspension had been viewed with suspicion until Moto Guzzi proved its worth in the 1930s seems incomprehensible now, as does the crudeness of plunger rear suspension. But plunger frames – with suspension units mounted either side of the rear axle – were easy and cheap adaptations to a rigid frame, whereas a swinging-arm frame required more substantial alterations and thus much more expense for the factory.

There was also a third significant difference between the Bullet and the other British factories' comparable offerings – the Bullet was designed as a 350, when even the ultimate British single, the Manx Norton, was only available as a 350 when offered as what amounted to a sleeved-down and short of stroke 500. This meant that it weighed the same as the 500, so was much heavier than necessary at around 315lb (143kg) even in racing trim, with the road-going equivalents close to 400lb (181kg) – and these were the epitome of sporting British singles. The reason that most factories did not worry about this was principally cost, but also because weight was not a particular issue on the fast, sweeping road-racing circuits of the day, let alone the public highway. But Wilson-Jones was thinking about off-road competition where every extra ounce fatigued both the rider and machine, and so even in road trim with lights the new Bullet was a mere 350lb (159kg). By comparison, a Matchless G3L weighed 30lb (14kg) more, while BSA's B31 was a whopping 60lb (27kg) heavier than the Enfield.

Enfield's newcomer also had a very different motor to its Model G predecessor. The ohv engine housed its dry sump's oil tank in a compartment in the crankcase, a long-time Enfield innovation. But previous Enfield singles had the tank in a crankcase that extended ahead of the cylinder base, giving the motors a distinctive jutting chin with a filler cap on the right. The new Bullet had the tank behind the crank, creating a more compact, modern silhouette. You can imagine

designer Tony Wilson-Jones thinking about bash plates and short wheelbases for his mud-plugging exploits.

Behind the crankcase was a four-speed Albion gearbox rigidly bolted on in a semi-unit style. The idea had first been seen on a prototype BSA A7, dubbed 'semi-unit' by BSA and flown to Paris in September 1946 for the first motorcycle show after the end of the war. Here, the crankcase and the gearbox were bolted to one another, with the gearbox in a fixed position. Primary chain adjustment was accomplished with a slipper-type tensioner inside the duplex chain's case, rather than by moving the gearbox relative to the crankcases – and embarking on a juggling act to get both primary and final drive-chain tension correct. Thus the semi-unit design not only made chain adjustment much easier, but also made for a much more rigid engine/gearbox structure, almost on a par with 'unit construction' types, where the gearbox and crankcase were one unit.

In contrast to other manufacturers, Enfield's patented cush drive in the rear wheel meant that the bikes could manage without an output shaft or clutch shock absorber, although the cush drive could make changing the rear sprocket a challenge.

While the innovative swing arm and telescopic forks were a great leap forward, the brakes are tiny even by the standards of the day, hinting at Royal Enfield's focus on off-road sport. BONHAMS

SMOOTH SPEED AND CUSHION COMFORT

Give yourself a big break, bring every road, track and lane to billiard table smoothness by riding a Royal Enfield "350 Bullet"; a spring frame motorcycle with perfected telescopic front fork and swinging arm type rear suspension giving lateral rigidity and eliminating strain on the wheel spindle. Please write for full particulars.

PRICE
"350 BULLET" £145-0-0
Plus Purchase Tax £39-3-0

Royal Enfield
By MILES the Best!

THE ENFIELD CYCLE CO LTD. Head Office & Works. REDDITCH.
LONDON SHOWROOMS AND SPARES DEPOT. 221. TOTTENHAM COURT ROAD. W.I.

Royal Enfield made much of the ability of the Bullet's suspension to make roads feel billiard-table smooth.

The Bullet could be had in road, trials, or scrambles versions, with equipment and gearing to suit the application, but the new prototype Bullet first broke ground as a 346cc trials bike, ridden by a works trio at the Colmore Cup Trial. The engine featured an RR56 light alloy con rod and a turned piston in low-expansion alloy. Unusually, Enfield used a floating bronze bush instead of a more conventional roller big-end bearing. Power was 18bhp at 5,750rpm, with the compression kept at a modest 6.5:1 to cope with the low-octane fuels of the era.

While unsuccessful on its initial outing, the newest Royal Enfield soon showed its form with Bullet-mounted riders winning gold medals later in 1948 in the ISDT, an important part of the winning British Trophy team. ISDTs would witness the debut of many new Royal Enfields in future, as we shall see in Chapter 9.

That the Bullet went so well off-road surprised many, because not everyone agreed that a rear swinging arm was a good idea. But the criticism was based upon the poor damping of the early adopters, which kept the rear wheel hopping as it bounced over the rocks and gullies. Until the Bullet, trials bikes had rigid rear frames, favoured for their light weight and predictable handling, with competitors relying on exceptional throttle control, a perfect sense of balance, a cool head, strong thighs and low down torque.

So the new Bullet attracted much attention when the public finally got to see it at the 1948 Earl's Court Show in London. Its 'exclusive features' included: a detachable rear mudguard; Enfield's rubber-block cush drive, which 'smooths out chain snatch and adds considerably to the life of both chain and tyres'; the spring frame, which 'supplies perfect lateral rigidity without increasing wheelbase or weight'; the gearbox's neutral finder; and a 'scientifically designed' air cleaner.

The trials models were 'specially tuned to meet the requirements of the trials rider with low compression pistons, small bore carburettors and heavier flywheels … an efficient air filter and Lucas Wader magneto'. But the prototype's aluminium alloy barrels with iron liners were replaced with cast-iron items for production, set deeply into the crankcases for good thermal conduction and cooling, and also for strength: along with the semi-unit gearbox this ensured great chassis rigidity. The power train was a stressed member of a lightweight frame that had only a single front down tube and a single saddle post with a looped subframe for the rear shock absorbers.

And so in 1949 the Bullet went on sale at £171 9s, while the old rigid Model G was still offered at £146. The trials and scrambler versions lacked the air cleaner and neutral finder, but gained aluminium alloy – rather than pressed-steel – mudguards, further lightened on the scrambler, which had a straight-through exhaust. It also had a close-ratio gearbox and a choice of compression ratios. The trial version had a wide-ratio gearbox, but all three models cost the same. The following year brought inevitable tweaks, most notably a longer, more powerful dynamo (60W, up from 40), while 1951 saw the timing-side crankshaft bush supplemented by a caged roller race. Oil feed was also upgraded.

However, although the early G2 Bullet was well engineered, well finished and well thought out, it was not especially well received. The press of the day would damn it with faint praise. *The Motor Cycle* in 1950 admired the suspension, low fuel consumption and affordability for youngsters, but suggested that a more experienced rider would find it 'basic', and principally a ride to work machine. Compared to sportier (and 500cc singles especially) roadsters, the Bullet sold poorly, overshadowed by the equivalent offerings from Triumph, BSA and Norton. Those motorcycles were better looking, faster and, given competition success, captured the imagination – and pay cheques – of the nation's youth. A 500 was also more suited to pulling a sidecar, still the only serious proposition for British families desirous of powered personal transport.

So, while another tester suggested that the 350 Bullet was plenty on Britain's 'crowded' roads – if only he could have foreseen today's congestion – and that a 500cc machine was only really needed overseas in more open lands, he was being prescient. When Royal Enfield stretched the Bullet to 499cc, it was overseas markets it was targeting, but not for the reasons suggested in the road test.

THE BULLET 500

Britain's trade deficit – the gap between the value of what was exported and imported – had been growing since the mid-1930s and World War II effectively brought overseas sales to an end, while the country imported everything from food to fighter aircraft. In 1941, Britain and the United States signed the Atlantic Charter, expressing the ideal of free trade, yet, by the end of the war, Britain had lost two-thirds of its export markets and was having to rely upon American loans as well as repaying the wartime lease-lend arrangements. With the Empire fading fast, there was really only one market to look toward – the United States itself.

Furthermore, nationalization meant that British steel production was under government control, a government that, from 1947, insisted that steel would only be available to businesses that exported at least 75 per cent of their production. How strictly this was applied is moot, but the message was simple: export or die. And while the Americans loved an off-road, single-cylinder British motorcycle, it was usually a BSA and always a 500. They also loved a big twin, but that's for another chapter.

So in 1952, the 499cc (usually referred to as the 500) Model JS Bullet went into production. The stroke was the same as the 350 G2 Bullet at 90mm, but bored out to 84mm from the original 70mm. Almost identical to its smaller brother, the 500cc Bullet featured a larger rear brake (7in versus 6in), different lighting and revised front fork legs with increased trail, hinting at sidecar use, but initially for 'export markets' – read the United States – only.

The November 1952 Motorcycle Show at Earls Court was the British public's first chance to see the new 500 and to place orders for delivery the following year. There were changes that would be shared with the 350, most noticeable the winged metal tank badge, but it was 1954 that saw the big changes. This introduced a cast-alloy headlamp casing enclosing the top yoke, speedometer, headlight and pilot

A 1953 Bullet 500.
BONHAMS

This Bullet 500 was ridden in the 1967 ISDT in Poland by Welsh motorcycling stalwart, William Basil 'Billy' Mills. Billy competed in a variety of off-road disciplines throughout the 1950s and 1960s. BONHAMS

lights, which would have been called a nacelle by anybody else, but Royal Enfield insisted it was a 'casquette' – French for a cap with a peak.

Inside the engine there were changes to the engine breather, which switched from a timed system venting to the atmosphere, to an elbow pipe aiming the oil mist at the drive sprocket and chain. The Bullet's gear-box end cover was also redesigned with a simpler casting, and with the gear lever and kick-start now pivoting on a shared axis.

A 1959 Big Head 499cc Bullet. BONHAMS

Another 1959 Big Head Bullet showing off the famous headlight casquette with pilot lights. BONHAMS

In 1955, dual seats, optional since 1952, became a standard fitment. As fuel quality improved, the 350's compression was raised to 7.25:1, which, together with a new camshaft and other modifications, took the claimed power from 18bhp to 19.5bhp; 20bhp according to some reports. With a light redesign and retooling at the Redditch plant, the Bullet's modernization programme advanced apace. Frames were upgraded, most obviously with bracing around the shock absorber's mounts, and the 500's swing arm was widened to allow a broader tyre. Both bikes gained twin 6in front brake hubs from the 672cc Meteor twin, which had been an option in 1954. Although tricky to set up, when correctly aligned these could be a vast improvement on what was available elsewhere. There were also cast-alloy fork sliders from the Meteor. The 350 Bullet gained a re-ported cylinder head with a larger inlet valve, with the exhaust header pipe now a push fit instead of a push-over stub. Cooling fins were cast into the oil tank section of the crankcase. The main bearings were changed, giving a ball race and roller on the drive side, with a double roller on the timing side. The timing side plain bearing, however, remained.

'This is the bike that you can rely on to get you there – and back!' boasted Royal Enfield's advertising. Even the 350 Bullet was considered suitable for a jaunt to 'the Scottish Highlands or to any other place where rough road surfaces, adverse weather conditions and tough going prevail. The stamina and endurance of the spring frame model has proved itself the world over.'

It was this 1955 version of the 350 Bullet that was sent from the Redditch factory in kit form for assembly in India, the legacy of a 1952 order from the Indian Army for border patrol use, but that story is for a later chapter.

UPDATES AND THE WORKS REPLICA

Between 1956 and 1960, the British Bullet was released in several models, including a 350cc 'works replica', based on trials superstar Johnny Brittain's machine, but again that's for a later chapter.

A welded, rather than brazed lug, frame also arrived for 1956, with rear shocks updated to Armstrong units giving 3in (76mm) of travel and much improving the handling according to contemporary road tests. The 350 motor gained a bigger Monobloc carb and a further compression boost to 7.75:1, plus a new exhaust system. The 350's constant tweaks, inherited from the Super Meteor, meant that it was now almost as quick

The Airflow fairing and mudguard was an expensive option, but was even available for the small two-stroke models.

Another view of the Big Head 500; the large cylinder head that gave the model its name is obvious. BONHAMS

as the 500, both being tested at around 80mph (129km/h) flat out, with the 350 now a free-revving unit compared to the lazier 500. Perhaps counter-intuitively, many preferred the 350 because of this, but both models were in the twilight of their years and Royal Enfield needed to develop a 250cc range. This was important and urgent, with an eye on changes to UK legislation that would limit new riders (albeit still allowed a provisional licence at sixteen years old) to a motorcycle with no more than 250cc from 1960, and a requirement to display 'L' (learner) plates until the perfunctory test was passed. The legislation would also lead to a short-lived and unpopular new unit-construction Bullet – in name rather than in the tradition of the 350 – built from 1963 until 1965 and based upon the firm's unit-construction 250 range.

In 1958, the Airflow version of the Bullet offered full weather protection with a large fibreglass fairing and also included panniers for touring. The design was developed in partnership with British Plastics and was featured as a series of articles in *The Motor Cycle* magazine. There were also minor differences to exhaust, seating, instrumentation, handlebars and fuel tank.

There was a last gasp for the original Bullet in 1959, the most significant change being for the 500cc version and the introduction of the Big Head. With integral rocker boxes and a downdraught carburettor, Enfield was making a genuine, if rather late, attempt to grab a slice of the sales of BSA's Gold Star. In a similar vein, cam profiles were revised with a higher lift, which riders used to the Bullet's all-road rather than sporting character did not really like, while the updated 500 seemingly failed to take any Gold Star sales at all.

Another questionable upgrade was the change to 17in wheels – down from the classic 19in – on the 350cc Bullet, again to the disappointment of traditional Royal Enfield buyers. In truth this was rationalization as Royal Enfield geared up for 250 production, those models being designed around 17in wheels. For 1960, magnetos were phased out as Lucas abandoned production and coil ignition replaced them. Further rationalization saw the 500cc Bullet revert to dual 6in front brakes, while the 350 gained the 7in single full-width drum from the Crusader Sports 250.

The following years saw few changes, probably because both machines were not long for the catalogue and there was little sense in investing in the semi-unit singles that looked increasingly dated compared to the unit-construction 250 singles from BSA and Royal Enfield itself.

In 1962, following the death of Major Smith, the UK company was sold and the Bullet, in both the 346cc G2 and 499cc JS guises, was discontinued. Both had served the firm well for almost fifteen years, having steadily, if never dramatically, clocked up sales, and their demise brought to an end the era

of British-made Bullets. The final fling was the 1963 New Bullet, effectively a 250 Crusader stretched to the original's 70 × 90mm bore and stroke and 346cc. With 7.5:1 compression giving a claimed 22bhp at 6,500rpm propelling a lightweight 310lb (141kg), better sales might have been hoped for, but it never so much as covered its development costs. Riders were either limited to 250cc, or looking to jump to the big time. The day of the 350, in the UK at least, seemed to be passing.

But way back in 1952, when Frank Sheene – Barry's father – had ridden a 350 Bullet to sixtieth place in the Junior TT, India's Royal Enfield importers Madras Motors had received an order from the Indian Army for 800 350cc Bullets. The motorcycles arrived from Redditch in early 1953 and were a great success, being both reliable and easy to maintain. It would prove to be a pivotal moment and produce a unique rescue story for the British motorcycle industry.

Drive-side view of the Big Head Bullet 500. BONHAMS

Contrast the **Big Head 500** motor with this early trials **Bullet 350. BONHAMS**

THE OTHER SINGLES

6

The reason that the Bullet created such a furore in 1948 was that most motorcycles on sale in the aftermath of World War II, as production of civilian machines gradually restarted, were just reheated 1930s basics, built with a lack of ambition that would lead to most of them eventually being lumped into what motorcyclists called the 'grey porridge' category: they did the job, but without much joy. But what was unappreciated by the baby boomers' generation was how hard life had been. As I grew older I realized that for all the grumbling about the 1970s – strikes, power cuts, dizzying

One of the first civilian Royal Enfields post-World War II, the twin-port 500 Model J. BONHAMS

The Model G and Model J models were revived pre-war designs and featured a rigid rear frame and a four-speed Albion gearbox. The J featured telescopic forks and a twin-port 499cc engine (84 × 90mm bore and stroke) and a 5.5:1 compression ratio, and used an Amal 276 side-bowl carburettor and Lucas magneto ignition. BONHAMS

inflation and village life dying as mechanization replaced farm labour – to people living just twenty years before, our lives would have looked the stuff of dreams.

Hard winters saw villages cut off for weeks, explaining why our elders lived in houses stuffed to the rafters with tinned food and garden sheds full of coal, and we have seen how quickly that mentality resurfaces in time of crisis. Old rod-braked bikes were everywhere, often free to a good home, because the only work was several miles away and buses made their solitary appearances for market-day trips and on Saturdays. Villages and towns were punctuated with forbidding homes behind tall hedges where Mrs (or often Miss) Long-Forgotten lived alone, widowed or spinstered at an early age by men who never returned from war. It was this world that newly available personal transport was born into, a world where men seeking work had little beyond a demob suit and a half-remembered hero's welcome.

So as the dust settled on war, even the most basic motorcycle was salvation, a way into work, rest and play. Affordable (just, on Easy Terms), and genuinely capable of perhaps as much as 100mpg (2.83ltr/100km), this was how post-war Britain got moving. The idea of being able to buy a refurbished – let alone a brand new – motorcycle had been unimaginable until World War II finally reached its grizzly conclusion in the Far East. And all Royal Enfield could initially offer was motorcycles that had been designed a decade before, when the 1936 range with vertical cylinders began to be phased in. The first of these new machines were the ohv models G (350cc) and J (500cc), both of which came with coil ignition, dry-sump lubrication and four-speed foot-change gearboxes. Later in the year the line-up expanded to include the basically similar 250cc ohv S2 and 350cc side-valve Model C.

In 1940, the WD (War Department) military Model C commenced delivery to UK armed forces and approximately 17,600 had been produced before the model was superseded by the ohv WD/CO in 1942. By the war's end more than 29,000 WD/C and WD/CO models had been built, many still held at the Redditch factory when hostilities ceased, and these were swiftly refurbished and sold as 'rebuilt WD machines' – effectively repainted and checked over old stock – during the late 1940s. These included the Flying Flea, finally listed as the RE 125cc and, alongside the 250s, also repurposed at the Bradford-on-Avon works. Like many others, Royal Enfield needed quickly to replace the War Department orders with those from the general public.

Beyond this, by late 1946 Royal Enfield could offer three related models, effectively pre-war continuations: the G, J and C/CO. The G and J were of 346cc and 499cc respectively and used the same ohv engine, the G with Enfield's classic 70 × 90mm bore and stroke; the J was enlarged with an 84mm bore. The CO used the G motor and the C likewise, but with side, rather than overhead, valves. Models G and J had a new telescopic front fork, whereas the C/CO retained the pre-war girders. All had cast-iron barrels and heads, plain big-end bearings, four-speed Albion gearboxes featuring Enfield's characteristic neutral selector lever, and rigid frames. But demand was still so great compared to production, and such was the pressure to export, that even the

first catalogue post-war for 1947 only listed the RE 125cc and the 350 Model G, the latter described thus: 'As a fast touring machine deluxe the 350cc ohv has no equal. The engine provides plenty of power and speed and is exceptionally smooth and sweet, even on Pool petrol.'

The telescopic forks were highlighted, as were Royal Enfield's war efforts. The Redditch factory also boasted of the competition successes of 1946, although most of those were with prototype Bullets. There is no mention of the Bradford-on-Avon facilities, possibly because they remained secret and were producing the diesel generators at least for the government. The only other things listed for sale were optional leg shields and speedometers: if you could forgo these, the RE 125cc was £73 13s 3d and the Model G £146 1s, both including purchase tax at a whopping 27 per cent. This was at a time when £100 a year was a typical annual income for a working man, although this illustrates the danger of comparing prices over the years: with inflation, £73 in 1948 equates to around £2,500 now, but average full-time incomes are far more generous than the £3,500 to which 1948's £100 is now equivalent. So even a new RE 125cc represented a huge chunk of most people's wages, let alone the Model G. But it is easy to understand why people still

The Model J2 was a 1949 update, but still retained an all-iron motor and rigid rear end. BONHAMS

ROYAL ENFIELD
MODEL R.E. 125 c.c.
TWO STROKE

The **RE 125 was a Flying Flea** for post-war Britain, offering affordable transport for the masses.

Originally designed as a light, easily-handled utility machine this amazing little mount proved its worth in the recent war when it was used by the Airborne Forces, who found it could be taken where it was impossible to take larger and heavier machines. The 125 c.c. machine is capable of long journeys even though its main function is that of an economical lightweight runabout.

aspired to two wheels rather than four: according to *Motor* magazine in October 1948, the Ford Anglia was the cheapest car in Britain at around £300. And that would only do some 30mpg (9.4ltr/100km) and carried all the other costs associated with running a car, which were far greater than the cost of running a motorcycle.

However, at least the RE and Model G were available; the Model J with a full 499cc was only available in export markets initially. In 1948, it was joined by the J2, virtually identical bar a twin-port head, with exhaust pipes on both sides of the motorcycle. This was the year that Royal Enfield launched its first twin-cylinder motor since the demise of the V-twins, and the J2 could bask in the reflected glory of the new 500 vertical parallel twin, imaginatively dubbed 500 Twin. This would be the start of a line of parallel twins that lasted until the demise of the Westwood factory at Bradford-on-Avon in 1970 that is detailed in Chapter 8.

THE FLYING FLEA DEMOBS FOR CIVILIAN LIFE

The DKW motor that had been adapted to create the Royal Baby 125 and then the wartime Model WD-RE, better known as the Flying Flea, was an obvious basis for cheap post-war transport. Its close relative, the DKW RT125 (*Reichs Typ*, or National Model) was quick (a very relative term), reliable and cheap to buy and run. The war came and went, but the RT125 remained in production.

Unfortunately at war's end DKW's Zschopau factory found itself on Russia's side of Germany's new big fence (soon to become an Iron Curtain), but some wise heads at DKW fled westward and established a new workshop in Ingolstadt in Bavaria, north of Munich. As soon as the Allies gave the factory the green light the reborn and relocated DKW began building the first post-war RT125W, suffixed to show that it had been manufactured in the west. Its 123cc, long-stroke motor used an alloy head and an iron barrel and, crucially, a deflectorless piston. With a compression ratio of 5.9:1 claimed power was 4.75bhp at 5,000 rpm. Primary chain drive was to a three-speed gearbox and chain final drive. The design was good enough to survive most of the 1950s and much longer in what became East Germany. MZ built them, as did IFA (*Industrieverband Fahrzeugbau* – Industrial Association for Vehicle Construction) in the old Horch (another of the Auto Union's) factory in Zwickau. The Russian RT125 replicas were sold as the MIA Moskva and K-125. WFM of Poland also built a version (the SHL 125 and Sokół 125), developing into the 125/175cc family that survived until 1985.

But the Ingolstadt DKW factory need not have worried about keeping its design alive in the west. The Allies denied Germany any copyrights as part of war reparations and so, keen to develop an entry-level range, Harley-Davidson's Hummer 125 was a stateside take on the RT125W from 1955 to 1959. Meanwhile, Yamaha, having re-established its production of musical instruments, decided to use facilities left over from wartime production to diversify into motorcycles. The Yamaha Motor Company was established in 1955 to make an improved RT125W as the first Yamaha motorcycle, the YA-1 Red Dragonfly, from 1955 to 1958. But the version of the little Deek that we all remember is the one that BSA sold some 400,000 of – the Bantam. BSA actually produced a mirror image of the motor to ensure a traditional British right-foot gear change, where Royal Enfield simply used a linkage. After all, BSA was starting tooling from scratch for the home market, whereas Royal Enfield had originally intended the Royal Bay – now listed as the RE 125cc – to be sold by the Dutch DKW distribution Stokvis, as we saw at the beginning of Chapter 4. Oddly, the RE 125, like its predecessors the Royal Baby and Flying Flea, had a hand lever gear shift on the right, rather than the left-side foot change of the DKW.

It was odd that Enfield transposed the gear change for a motorcycle to be sold in the Netherlands and hints that the company intended to sell in the UK from the start. British motorcycles were almost unique in having a right-foot gear shift. The most plausible explanation is road camber: early European roads tended to be particularly cambered (that is, raised in the centre with gutters at the sides to clear rainfall), so that, sitting at the roadside waiting to pull away to drive on the left, it was easier to steady the bike with the left foot

and engage first gear with the right. If you drove on the right, as mostly everybody but the British did, the opposite was true. And in the days of hand shifts, a left-hand clutch meant that it was easiest to engage gears with the right hand, so updating to a foot shift would have been simplest and cheapest if it remained on the right.

At first, the Japanese manufacturers copied the British pattern – not only because some of their earlier bikes, like the Kawasaki W series, were based on British designs, but because they also drive on the left. However, as they expanded, they noted that most markets – and especially American riders – were used to a left-side shift, so, being an exporting nation, they adopted that pattern.

By the 1960s, safety campaigner Ralph Nader had decided that inexperienced or panicked riders might stamp on the gear shift when they wanted the back brake (still an important stopping aid back then), so he persuaded the US government that standardization was needed. Harley-Davidson supported the move to its preferred left-side shift, which would mean that British competitors would have to spend money and time on linkages to accommodate the law, spoiling a gear shift that was generally much slicker than on Harley-Davidsons. But in post-war Britain, a left-side gear shift was an anathema and potentially a disincentive to stick with a British motorcycle when graduating up the capacity ladder. But while at BSA the RT125's motor was redrawn as a perfect mirror image to ensure that the gear shift was on the 'correct' side, Royal Enfield was already geared up – literally – to build its 125 with a left-hand gear shift. With little cash to spare, the RE 125cc simply got a linkage for its three-speed gearbox.

At least this allowed Royal Enfield to undercut the Bantam by a whopping £2 and the RE was a little lighter and substantially more economical. But it was less powerful (3.5 vs 4bhp) and it was the Bantam that caught the public's imagination, with the RE needing an update sooner rather than later. Although the RE's DKW-style front girder forks were admired, the Bantam had telescopic forks and so, for 1950, the RE was similarly equipped. Like the Bantam's, these were undamped and without rebound springs, but still the RE sales disappointed. A racing version was developed with Bill Lomas and, while sales failed to take off, this at least helped to develop a replacement. In 1951, a new model was introduced, the RE2 now with a foot gear change, claiming a Bantam-bashing 4.5bhp, but 1953 was the last year of Enfield's 125.

THE ENSIGN AND THE PRINCE

In 1952, the tiny stroker grew from the RE's 124.8cc, via a bore and stroke of 53.8 × 55mm, to 56 × 60mm and 148cc. Compression also increased from 5.5 to 6.5:1 to claim 5.25bhp, while it would be another two years before BSA similarly stretched the Bantam. This was listed as the Ensign, with much greater comfort provided by a hybrid swinging arm and plunger rear suspension with springs. It was followed by the 1956 Ensign II, with larger forks, brakes and cylinder finning. A dual seat and chrome highlights immediately identified it as new and hidden changes within the motor made it quieter and faster. *The Motor Cycle* wrung 51mph (82km/h) and 96mpg (2.95ltr/100km) from Royal Enfield's new baby, concluding 'that the Ensign II is an outstanding machine in its class, relatively inexpensive to buy (£105 8s) and cheap to

run'. The following year saw the lighting upgraded and 1958 cosmetic tweaks and an Ensign II moniker, but these were not enough to save the Royal Enfield from being savaged by Bantams in the showroom.

So for 1959 there was another jump in power, now 7.5bhp at 4,750rpm, despite no increase in capacity and a completely new name: Prince. It was justified, for the Prince looked like a grown-up motorcycle with swinging-arm rear suspension, featuring damped Armstrong rear shock absorbers. A plumper dual seat and chunkier side panels and fuel tank added to the impression of a (comparatively) De Luxe commuter rather than basic transport. It now shared nothing beyond basic architecture with its origins as the Royal Baby, even the crankshaft now having proper flywheels rather than bob weights. *The Motor Cycle* admired 'a stylish lightweight combining smart appearance with excellent economy and

The 148cc Ensign was an attempt to update the RE 125. BONHAMS

150 Ensign

ENGINE-GEAR UNIT : New 148 c.c. engine unit of pleasing streamlined design. Foot-controlled three-speed gear. Clutch running at engine speed ensuring super-light operation. Miller generator and ignition system which ensures easy starting under all conditions. FRAME : Entirely new design, incorporating swinging arm rear suspension which gives complete absorption of road shocks. All main tubes of chrome molybdenum alloy steel. Easy lift, spring-up, centre stand. WHEELS : 2·75 × 19in. Dunlop tyres front and rear. Powerful 5in. brakes on both wheels. EXHAUST SYSTEM : Incorporates special stream-lined expansion chamber in addition to silencer. FINISH : Copper Beech Polychromatic enamel with bright parts heavily chromium plated. Attractive new tank transfer of modern design

Royal Enfield was clearly proud of the Ensign, but it could not compete with the BSA Bantam.

Royal Enfield

RAME MODELS FOR PERFECT SU

good all round performance'. At 110mpg (2.57ltr/100km), it was even more economical than the Ensign and a tad faster. But by 1962 the Prince was gone and Royal Enfield was in the middle of a change of ownership, blissfully unaware of the storm to come.

Royal Enfield – along with much of the British manufacturing industry – was unprepared for the revolution that was coming. While many countries sought to protect their domestic manufacturers, especially as they grew from tentative post-war rebirth, the British were welcoming open trade in a remarkable turn of laissez-faire. Chief among these was the Anglo-Japan agreement of 1962, which gave the Japanese almost unrestricted and immediate access to the UK market in return for little or nothing; certainly not access to the Japanese market. This was seen as a diplomatic

and generous offer to a broken nation that deserved help in rebuilding. In reality, Edward Turner's well-documented tour of the Japanese factories two years earlier should have served as a stark warning to British industry to remove the government's rose-tinted glasses. Instead, the industry continued to wear its own pink-gin spectacles, believing that the Japanese lightweights would help to expand the market for motorcycles in general and large capacity British twins in particular. Royal Enfield was happy to drop the lightweights and focus on the 250cc domestic market, fuelled by the UK's learner rider limits, and exporting big twins to America. The UK motorcycle market had already peaked in 1959 and British motorcycle manufacturers turned once again to the US market to maintain sales and profitability. Then in 1962 the Enfield Cycle Company was purchased by E. & H.P.

A major update followed for the Ensign to become a proper lightweight motorcycle as the Prince.

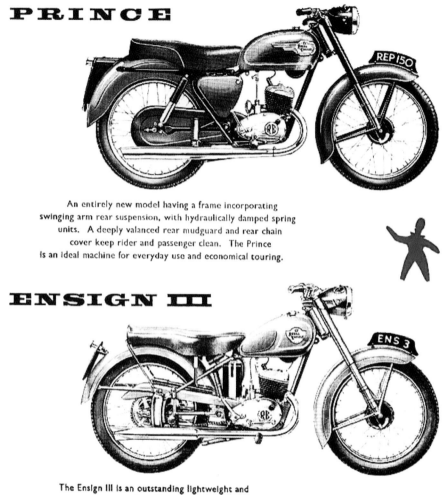

PRINCE

An entirely new model having a frame incorporating swinging arm rear suspension, with hydraulically damped spring units. A deeply valanced rear mudguard and rear chain cover keep rider and passenger clean. The Prince is an ideal machine for everyday use and economical touring.

ENSIGN III

The Ensign III is an outstanding lightweight and gives comfortable and economical running at speeds up to 55 m.p.h.

Smith, who also owned Alpha Bearings, at just the point where ready cash, a deep understanding of the motorcycling world and exemplary management were needed. As change came, employees quickly realized all was not well, but again that's for a later chapter. In the meantime there's a different sort of fury to consider.

THE FURY FLAT TRACKER

In 1932, the American Motorcyclist Association (AMA) sanctioned a new Dirt Track championship, with manufacturers inevitably entering prototype machinery. So, for the following year, the AMA introduced a new class that only allowed production motorcycles in an effort to attract owner-riders and increase entries: this being America, profit was paramount and organizers wanted as many spectators as possible. And then came the Great Depression, a collapse in factory entries and the production class – Class C – became the most important championship by far, a situation that rapidly became the norm, even as World War II ended and the post-war boom began.

Presumably with an eye on British motorcycles competing, the AMA ruled that side-valve engines should displace no more than 750cc – in other words, Harley-Davidson and Indian V-twins – while ohv engines were limited to 500cc.

The Fury was another attempt to win over **BSA** customers, this time in **US** off-road sport. BONHAMS

This **Fury has been converted for road use, as many were, usually with full lighting kits.** BONHAMS

A period **US TT competitor with a Fury.** A HERL INC

Pretty much all sporting British motorcycles had overhead valves and most were motors with no more than 500cc.

In 1954, the Grand National Championship series was introduced featuring four different types of competitions: three of the competitions (Mile, Half-mile, TT) were held on dirt tracks, while the fourth was held on asphalt. When Indian closed its doors in 1953, the Harley-Davidson factory was left to dominate the series until, in the 1960s, the British arrived in force. Dick Mann won the national title for BSA in 1963, marking the first victory for a foreign manufacturer. Triumph would win three Grand National championships in four years, with Gary Nixon winning back to back titles in 1967 and 1968. Royal Enfield understandably noticed this and wanted a piece of the action.

Like BSA and Triumph, Royal Enfield had big twins to sell into the US market, with the top flight models all over 500cc. Limited to that capacity, the singles actually had better traction on dirt than the twins and it was also a chance for the Brits to sell their singles into the huge off-road market. So BSA raced the Gold Star rather than the A7 twin, while Royal Enfield built a unique model rather than race its 500 Twin.

Enter the Fury. This competition model was built expressly for the US flat-track competition market. It was essentially a Bullet 500 bottom end with a substantially larger and unique cylinder head with extra finning, an integrated rocker box, larger ports and inlet valve. The bike was nicknamed 'Big Head' after the larger top end of the motor, fed via a 1½in (38mm) Amal GP carburettor and running a Lucas N1 racing magneto. A Big Head Bullet was sold in the UK concurrently for the civilian market with a smaller inlet valve and Amal Monobloc carburettor.

The Fury was fitted with an Alfin aluminium alloy barrel with a cast-iron liner (instead of the Bullet's all-iron barrel), as had the prototype and some competition Bullets. Launched in 1959 as Royal Enfield's competitor to the BSA Gold Star and Velocette Venom sports singles, further engine tuning included raised compression (8.9:1 instead of 7.3:1) and lighter, rebalanced flywheels taken from the 350 Bullet. Maximum output for the 500 version was claimed at 40bhp (compared to the 500 Bullet's 27), with top speed listed as 'over 95mph' (153km/h). The front fork was fitted with stiffer competition springs and the Armstrong rear shock absorbers with two preload settings. Lights and a rev counter were optional; wheels were 19in front and 18in rear.

Only 191 Fury 500s were produced between 1959 and 1963 according to the factory's manufacturing records, although some claim that 193 were built if the dispatch records are correct. The main years of Fury production were 1959–60, with 156 500s plus a one-off run of ten 350cc versions leaving the factory. In the 1961 model year, eleven were dispatched, although the model year being September to August hardly seems relevant for this low a volume. In 1962, just four Furies were built and twenty-two in the following year. A 600cc prototype was also built, but once again Royal Enfield discovered that what people really wanted in a single-cylinder competition bike was a BSA Gold Star.

THOSE THAT ALSO SERVED – BICYCLES, LAWNMOWERS AND ELECTRIC CARS

The Enfield Cycle Co. Ltd, like other large manufacturers, was hit by the depression and to help keep the workforce busy, the company began to produce motor mowers in 1932, continuing production until 1940. The best known of the range was the Royal Enfield powered roller mower.

Production restarted after the war with Enfield's in-house two-stroke engines and continued until 1956. The range of models had 98cc, 148cc and 225cc engines with cutting blades from 12 to 20in (309–508mm). The larger models

Royal Enfield employees at a show, demonstrating the diversity of the product range, which included lawnmowers.
ROYAL ENFIELD

were intended for groundsmen to use on such surfaces as cricket pitches and bowling greens.

The bicycles continued, three friends taking a cycling holiday to Lapland in July 1951 on Royal Enfield Bullet 3 bicycles. Even following the buyout by E. & H.P. Smith, there was a new small 20in-wheel model that went on sale as the Revelation.

After the buyout, Enfield Industrial Engines, which built the small, two-cylinder diesels and later marine engines, was sold as the E. & H.P. Smith industrial combine gradually disposed of non-motorcycle production. Enfield Industrial Engines was bought by Giannis 'John' Goulandris and relocated to the Isle of Wight, becoming Enfield Automotive, based at Somerton works, Cowes. The original Enfield 456 electric car had been reputedly built in an old garage on Elm Road, Wimbledon, apparently under the direction of Massachusetts Institute of Technology Alumnus Constantine Adraktas.

Around this time, Goulandris also established Enfield Marine along the road at Fishbourne Creek. Here, during the early 1970s, a series of highly successful race-winning aluminium-hulled power boats were built, the most famous being Miss Enfield 2 and Enfield Avenger.

Under Constantine Adraktas's direction, Somerton works became home to the car that evolved to meet Enfield's contract. It also benefited from the input of talented engineer John Ackroyd, perhaps better known for his later work on the Thrust 1 and Thrust 2 land speed record cars. The Enfield 465 was a small two plus two seater electric car equipped with a 48V, 4.65bhp (3kW) electric motor. Bodywork was an ICI royal plastic monocoque, with the rear axle coming from a Bond Bug. Just three were built.

The UK's Electricity Council funded its successor, the Enfield 8000, also known as the Electric City Car. Similar to the 465, albeit with an 8bhp (6kW) motor and aluminium body, 120 Enfield 8000s were built on Syros in Greece in the mid-1970s, of which sixty-five were used by the Electricity Council and southern English electricity boards. Then Governor of California, Ronald Reagan, had three E8000ECCs brought to California in support of his Clean Air legislation. The company was incorporated into Neorion, also owned by Goulandris, and renamed Enfield-Neorion.

THE FUTURE'S BRIGHT?

When Royal Enfield was taken over by the E. & H.P. Smith conglomerate in 1962 after the death of Major Smith (no relation), who had led the company since the 1920s, things looked promising, initially at least. The new company claimed to be bringing in fresh capital and keen motorcyclist Leo Davenport was moved from E. & H.P. Smith to Redditch, joining Royal Enfield's own Major Vic Mountford. The pair had direct access to the directors of E. & H.P. Smith, with Davenport, an ex-racer, keen to rekindle Royal Enfield's racing programme, signing up the charismatic Geoff Duke to race a new GP5 250cc machine. But the effort was haemorrhaging cash at a time when sales were falling dramatically and it was then discovered that the buyout had been largely with shares and at perhaps half of Enfield's true value.

The GP5 was not beyond the prototype stage when, in November 1964, Major Mountford died. This left a vacuum that was soon filled by voices from E. & H.P. Smith arguing that Royal Enfield should be split up and sold off, in what sounded remarkably close to what we would call asset-stripping today. This was just a few years after Royal Enfield had launched a completely new range of 250s to take advantage of the change to UK legislation in the hope of dominating a hitherto non-existent market, in the UK at least.

THE 250s

In 1950, 5,012 people were killed on Britain's roads, about half the figure of a decade before when the blackouts had made road travel so lethal. But by 1960 the figure had risen to almost 7,000, despite there being just four million licensed vehicles. With bus journeys accounting for half of all travel, government had to start on a direction of travel that would bring the number of deaths on Britain's roads to well under 2,000 a year despite the huge jump in personal motorized transport.

In the 1950s, motorcycles were still lumped in with bicycles in statistics at 14 per cent of travel, less than rail, car, trucks or indeed anything else. But fatalities did get recorded separately and by 1960 a quarter of all fatalities on Britain's roads were attributed to motorcycles, with the figure constantly rising. The press was already obsessed with the rise of the post-war youth culture and kept motorcycle fatalities in the public eye, arguably culminating in February 1961 with the *Daily Mirror* giving over its entire front page to a picture

Circa 1954 Clipper, a pre-unit model from the era when 250s were very much economy transport. That changed when, without passing a test, riders were limited to a 250cc motorcycle. BONHAMS

of a motorcyclist – in full rocker regalia – under the headline 'Suicide Club'. The motorcycle was a Royal Enfield Meteor Minor Sport, an uprated 500 twin launched in 1960. At the beginning of that year anybody with sufficient funds could have ridden one on their sixteenth birthday, without any protective clothing or training.

So UK legislation was therefore passed to limit new riders (although still allowed a provisional licence at sixteen years old) to a motorcycle with no more than 250cc from 1960 and a requirement to display 'L' (learner) plates until the perfunctory test was passed. The legislation meant that Royal Enfield needed to develop a 250cc range, in order to take on an entirely new market. Hitherto, 250cc motorcycles had been regarded as cheap and rarely cheerful transport for those on a budget. Typically, a two-stroke would be used, often bought in from the likes of Villiers, with little concern for the sort of glamour and sporting prowess that teenagers desired. Such riders would go for a 500, or a 350 at the very least – except, from 1960, they couldn't, in the UK at least. Royal Enfield, like all the British factories, was going to need a 250 to catch a young man's fancy, perhaps a first for the industry. The vanguard of this would be the Crusader.

Interviewed in 1957 on the Crusader's genesis, Royal Enfield's chairman and managing director Major Smith confided that he had wanted a 250 with:

> The best possibilities for combining a brisk road potential, economical running ... Unit construction of engine and gearbox was an obvious requirement for a de luxe model of up to date conception, with the proviso that accessibility of engine and gear mechanism ... must not be inferior to that obtainable with separate units.

So this was the brief that draftsman Reg Thomas and chief engineer Tony Wilson-Jones worked to when creating the Crusader, announced to the world in August 1957 for delivery the following year. Claimed power was 13bhp at 5,750rpm, which was probably honest given the rapidly climbing claims from competitors: despite a less sporting specification, BSA would claim 2bhp more at 750rpm less than two years later for its C15.

Quite why the British motorcycle industry took so long to adopt unit construction (that is, the gearbox within the crankcase rather than as a separate bolted-on unit) is a mystery. While it is true that gearbox teeth break down oil more quickly than bearings, and that in unit construction the oil is shared between the gearbox and the crankshaft and con-rod bearings, necessitating regular oil changes, otherwise the advantages of unit construction are compelling: stronger engine and gearbox cases; less wear and adjustment to the primary drive; better oil tightness; and a more compact and easy to package power train. The Italians went to unit construction almost from the off, except for the factories that bought in engines, and therein probably lies the truth: it was easy to buy in engines and gearboxes and call yourself a motorcycle factory. Designing and building a motor in-house was far trickier.

Yet Britain's motorcycle industry was based, for the most part, in huge factories that often made their own nuts and bolts, never mind gearboxes. It was probably an attitude – accepting the status quo – and an attitude that would not survive the arrival of Japanese machines. These not only had unit construction, but also horizontally rather than vertically split crankcases that simplified assembly and reduced the chance of oil leaks. Yet, despite stealing a march on the competition by building the first unit-construction British motorcycle engine, the Crusader's crankcases remained vertically split. Perhaps it was because Royal Enfield, like the rest of the British motorcycle factories, had a highly skilled workforce. By contrast, the Japanese – and BMW – designed their motors so that they could be assembled by unskilled workers.

CRUSADING SPECIFICATION

The vertically split crankcase and gearbox castings still needed to be matched and drilled so that the crank and gearbox aligned, rather than dropped into a pre-prepared bottom half of a horizontally split crankcase. The new Crusader's one-piece, cast-iron crank had a ball race bearing on the left-hand side and a roller on the right. The big end was a plain bearing to the RR56 alloy H-section con rod, with the gudgeon pin running directly in the con rod without a bush. The piston was a conventional full skirt, three-ring design. The cylinder head (initially cast iron, later aluminium alloy) had a hemispherical combustion chamber with what were considered large valves for the time – $1\frac{7}{16}$in (37mm) inlet and $1\frac{3}{8}$in (35mm) exhaust, clearance adjusted – unusually – at the top of the pushrods. The bore and stroke was also unusually over square at 70 × 64.5mm: BSA's C15 catch-up

CRUSADER 250

The luxury touring Crusader 250 is acknowledged as the outstanding machine of its class and gives smooth and safe motorcycling with exceptionally economical running. Crusader owners often record petrol consumption figures of well over 110 m.p.g.

The Crusader and new Clipper had new unit-construction 250cc motors and styling that might appeal to younger riders.

250 CLIPPER

The 250 Clipper, basically similar to the Crusader, has the same high standard of safety and stability which are the result of the low seating position and 17" wheels.
Exceptional economy in running and low initial cost make the 250 Clipper an outstanding utility machine.

was a rather more old-fashioned 67 × 70 mm, making it far less sporty. The carburettor was an Amal Monobloc ⅞in (22mm). The alternator and oil pump were on the right-hand side and a chain ran the camshaft with a slipper adjuster, rather like a miniature version of the primary drive, the high cam layout ultimately controlling the overhead valves via alloy pushrods.

Between the crankcase and gearbox was a 3pt (1.7ltr) oil tank cast within the crankcases, as was Royal Enfield's wont. An oil feed here lubricated the primary drive chain to the gearbox. Unusually, the lay shaft was behind the main shaft, there being plenty of space for the unit-construction motor compared to the preceding Bullet and the Clipper

(see below). It also allowed a more ergonomic positioning of the gear lever. The gear cluster remained an Albion unit, but the positive stop mechanism was Enfield's and the design was intended to allow much of the motor to be disassembled without removal from the frame. The clutch had three plates.

The all-welded steel frame was light and, with an all-new chassis and poised on slight 17in wheels, it was easy for a new rider to handle. The styling was stocky yet stylish, despite a huge and deeply valanced front mudguard.

Royal Enfield, soon joined by its fellow British factories, saw the restriction of learner motorcyclists to 250cc as a uniquely British opportunity. Suddenly there was a market

250 CRUSADER SPORTS

A really striking 250 having an output of 17 b.h.p., and a maximum speed of about 80 m.p.h. The engine is fitted with a light alloy cylinder head, large inlet valve, special two-rate valve springs, light alloy spring collars and push rods, special racing cams and high compression piston. The massive crankshaft carried on large diameter ball and roller bearings, and the short, very stiff, connecting rod form a sound foundation for the high revolutions and power output. A handsome tank and plated mudguards give the Crusader "Sports" an attractive and sporting appearance.

Royal Enfield

The Crusader Sport was very much an attempt to appeal to learner riders seeking glamour and performance.

Airflow

Airflow models are available in the following finishes : Ensign III and Prince, 250 Clipper, 350 Clipper, Meteor Minor Standard, *Cherry Red or Surf Green.*

Crusader 250, Crusader Sports, 350 and 500 Bullets, Meteor Minor De Luxe, Super Meteor and Constellation. *Polychromatic Burgundy or Peacock Blue.*

Any current Royal Enfield machine can now be fitted with "Airflow." The superbly styled fairing and front wheel guard, which are made from fibre-glass reinforced polyester resin, give as near 100% weather protection as is possible on a two wheeled vehicle. The "normally seated" maximum speed of the machine is increased by 5%–8% when Airflow is fitted, with an improvement of 20% in petrol consumption. For the touring rider or the "road burner" the Airflow takes the sting out of bad weather riding, and permits higher average speeds in perfect comfort and with complete weather protection.

Royal Enfield

The Airflow upgrade made Royal Enfield's 250s the most expensive on the market by far.

for sporty as well as budget 250s, doubling the potential market. There was also the likelihood that if the sporty models could attract a buyer with a provisional licence once they had passed their test – which would not only allow access to larger, faster models, but also to carrying a pillion passenger – the rider would trade up to a larger motorcycle from the same marque. Getting the new 250s right was important.

A FIRST – THE AIRFLOW FAIRING

The Crusader was available in Airflow form, with a large fibreglass fairing and matching front mudguard, a first for a mass-produced British motorcycle. Some very fancy claims were made to the press, which gave rise to much publicity, even if the *Daily Mail* referred to it as the Overflow rather than Airflow. Royal Enfield had form with fairings, having

shown the twin-headlight Bullet Dreamliner prototype in 1956, with a huge fairing that, sadly, never saw production.

But the Airflow did make production, available on the Bullet and Meteor twin as well as the Crusader, and the press release came with a photograph of a dashing rider on a 500 Bullet in the wind tunnel at Filton, just outside Bristol, where Concorde would be developed a decade later. The picture seemed to document a turning point in motorcycle design, the caption being dated 31 October 1958, although it is unclear whether that was the date of the test, or the date of the press release. A similar photograph of the motorcycle being readied for testing in the wind tunnel appears in the 6 November 1958 edition of *Motor Cycling*, the caption claiming that 'Extensive testing in laboratory, workshop and wind tunnel lies behind the Bristol-made Royal Enfield fairing. Our photograph shows an example being prepared for 90mph tests in one of the tunnels at Filton, Bristol.'

Royal Enfield did in fact make substantial claims for the Airflow. In the *Daily Mail* story, the factory boasted of an '8 per cent top-speed improvement' and a 20 per cent reduction in fuel consumption. There was even a glove box. Another article went so far as to claim that the Airflow provided helmet-like protection to the rider's body in a crash, the *Daily Mail* quoting the Major thus: 'The best features of the safe, honest-to-goodness motor-cycle and the stylish-looking scooter converge in this new design of ours.' Sadly, as Roy Bacon noted in his book, *Royal Enfield, the Postwar Models*: 'For a while it looked as if the public would follow this trend to combine motorcycle handling with scooter protection, but in a short space of time it was to reverse. Scooters were to fade from the scene and motorcycles went down the café-racer route to clip-ons and rear-sets.'

Next to this was the truth that results from the wind tunnel were dreadful. Tufts of wool taped to the motorcycle fairing did not show that the fairing worked. Wind-tunnel workers vetoed a suggestion that the tufts be further taped down in a convincing way to make a better photo. The final nail in the Airflow Crusader's coffin was the price: it added £44 to the Crusader's £212 1s 6d price tag (over 20 per cent more) to make it the most expensive British 250 you could – but almost certainly wouldn't – buy.

The publicity shot of an Airflow fairing in the wind tunnel at Filton, close to Bristol. A HERL INC

This superbly styled fairing made from glass fibre reinforced polyester resin, gives as near 100% weather protection as is possible on a two-wheeled vehicle. Available as original equipment on all current Royal Enfield machines except the Super 5, the Airflow actually increases overall performance and gives up to 20% improvement in petrol consumption.

The advertising was certainly colourful and the Sportflow fairing was more to the taste of young riders limited to a 250.

Exclusive to Royal Enfield "250" owners, this race-tailored aerodynamically designed fairing gives weather protection and increased performance, together with a truly sporting and fashionable appearance.
Easily fitted in a very short time the "Sportsflow" is supplied in matching colours for your model. Also available in white.

GUARANTEE
All Royal Enfield Motor Cycles are sold by our Dealers subject to the limited Guarantee adopted by the British Cycle and Motor Cycle Industries Association Ltd. Shortage of space prevents it being printed in full in this leaflet, but a copy will be sent on application. Specifications in this publication are subject to alteration at any time without notice.

The Enfield Cycle Co. Ltd.
Redditch
Worcestershire
England

Telephone:
REDDITCH 4222 (9 lines)
Telegrams:
"Cycles, Phone, Redditch"

820/50M/BBP. KNP./1162

ECONOMY CLASS – THE CLIPPER

The Clipper model name was used post-war by Royal Enfield for the economy versions of existing models and parts bins specials. The earlier Clippers were essentially Bullets offered with Model G motors or a version of the pre-war 250cc Model S. Both of these bikes were distinguished by having their oil tanks in front of the crankshaft rather than behind as for the newer models, with the motors being all iron instead of having alloy heads. Perhaps Royal Enfield was trying to use up overstocked parts in creating the Clippers, and may have expanded its market share by producing cheaper motorcycles, but equally many have argued that this was counterproductive when the company should have been seen as the upmarket, small-scale alternative to the big British factories.

The later 250cc Clipper, or Clipper II as it is sometimes known, appeared in 1958 to all intents and purposes as a Crusader, with the earlier cast-iron cylinder head instead of aluminium alloy, a smaller carburettor and a single saddle. It was rumoured that the prototype with an iron head had the same carburettor as the more expensive Crusaders, but actually ran better than its more expensive siblings, so Royal Enfield built the production version with a smaller carburettor to rein in performance and make sure that the higher price of the Crusader seemed justified.

Sadly, both the Royal Enfield 250 Crusader and its twin-cylinder competitor, the Norton Jubilee, quickly suffered from reputations for leaking oil and poor reliability, with the Norton offering hardly any more power than the best-selling of the new British 250s, the C15 – 16bhp versus 15bhp – despite weighing rather more. The Crusader's claimed 13bhp also now looked rather underwhelming, so for the 1959 model year there was the Crusader Sports, which would prove to be Royal Enfield's bestselling 250. Predating Roy Bacon's comments by decades, with more brightwork and dropped handlebars, the Sports' stance hinted at changes within the motor that would justify the café racer looks. A hotter cam, enlarged inlet valve, from $1^7/_{16}$in (37mm) to $1^9/_{16}$in (40mm) in an aluminium alloy head, increased compression (8 to 8.5:1) and a Monobloc $^7/_8$in (22mm) 376 carburettor gave a claimed 18bhp at 6,250rpm and an 80mph (129km/h) top speed.

Unfortunately, 1959 also marked Honda's arrival in the UK, with the company's famous Isle of Man debut.

THE ARRIVAL OF HONDA

The Crusader Sports' 18bhp seemed impressive in isolation – even Triumph's 350 twin only claimed 18.5bhp – but this would seem almost laughable in the face of Honda's 1961 CB77 305cc Super Hawk's 28bhp. Honda's 250 version, the CB72, might have given a little less, but it was still far better specified than any British motorcycle of whatever capacity. American author Aaron Frank called these 'the first modern Japanese motorcycles', and their credibility was assured when Elvis Presley rode a CB77 in the film

Roustabout. Loyalty, styling and credibility kept customers coming back to the British bikes to start with, but, with most at the top of British industry thinking of retirement rather than where the business might be in a decade or more, the end was in sight for anyone who cared to look for it. The huge loss of life in the recent war meant that there were also few middle managers waiting to take over the reins after years of gaining experience.

Gerald Davison was with Honda UK from 1968 to 1985, gaining influence and experience in every aspect of the business and becoming Honda's first non-Japanese director in the process. He had a reputation for single-mindedness and making sure that Honda was top dog – at races, market share, everything – regardless of what it took. Yet if you only ever knew him in the last few decades, you would find this hard to believe of the old school gentleman he now is, with a fine appreciation of antiques and a world-leading knowledge of Chinese ceramics. He'd already worked at Chrysler, moving to Honda at just age twenty-six. There was little or no competition:

> We had a completely different outlook. I didn't wear a suit, I wore a sports jacket. I didn't want to look like my father. When the job at Chrysler came up I knew they'd be looking for someone twice my age but rung up anyway. I was qualified for the job and, I suppose, had little competition. But I like to think I proved I could do it.

The British 'old boy network' did not see the new breed of hungry and ambitious young men from around the world as competition. Along with much of its manufacturing industry, Britain was unprepared for the revolution that was coming. While many countries sought to protect their domestic manufacturers, especially as they grew from tentative post-war rebirth, the British were welcoming open trade in a remarkable turn of laissez-faire. The industry continued to believe that the Japanese and European lightweights would help to expand the market for motorcycles in general and large capacity British twins in particular.

How wrong they were. In 1959, Bill Smith's focus was Grands Prix racing on works AJS and Matchless singles for the Arter team. In the Isle of Man he was introduced to Kawashima San, the new Honda team boss who would go on to become Honda President. Although others questioned Honda's four valve heads – a pre-war idea many felt – and newspaper reports suggested that Honda was a long way behind the Europeans because they had to work Saturdays and Sundays, Bill was one of the few to see potential. Never mind the RC141 and RC142 racers, the CB92 Benly roadsters that the teams were practising on might have been from another planet. A 125 with twin cylinders, ohc and electric start was unbelievable. Yet Bill was one of the few not to scoff, but to realize this was the future.

Bill had opened Bill Smith Motors Ltd in 1959 in Chester, north-west England, initially selling second-hand cars. But his contact with Honda led to a ride on a works 125cc Honda for the British Championships meeting at Oulton Park, finishing second to Mike Hailwood. Bill became determined to get involved with Honda and, in 1961, became the first to import Honda motorcycles into the UK. His bridgehead meant that he was offered the British concession, but with a catch: he was required to commit to taking 5,000 motorcycles a year. This was a huge number, although Honda's ambition was to sell 5,000 motorcycles a month in the United States. Still racing full time, Bill could not commit to such a total, so in 1962 Honda UK was formed. At the 1962 Earls Court Motorcycle Show Honda took orders for 26,000 motorcycles. To put that in perspective the world's biggest motorcycle factory, before Honda took over the title in the 1950s, spent much of World War II focused on building one model – the 350cc BSA M20 – and produced 125,000 of them over several years to ship across the planet. Yet BSA's reaction to Honda was, like subsidiary Triumph, bordering on gratitude, happy to see them grow the lightweight market and create a new generation of enthusiasts who would graduate to the big, bad British twins.

TWO-STROKE FIGHTBACK – THE ROYAL ENFIELD TURBO TWIN

Royal Enfield, to the company's credit, as well as developing its own big twin, refocused on the 250 market in 1964 with a completely new model, the 250cc Turbo Twin, Royal Enfield's answer to the Japanese two-stroke invaders. It featured the Villiers 4T twin-cylinder engine with a higher compression ratio of 8.75:1 than the previous Villiers engines. With a four-speed gearbox, the unit offered 17bhp and, married to the Crusader frame, Enfield hoped to produce

The Turbo Twin was an attempt to create a quality two-stroke 250 sportster. STEVE SMITH

a 70-plus mph (113km/h) machine with great handling. Early road tests confirmed that this had been achieved, with one publication declaring that 'firm springing and low centre of gravity make bend-swinging a pleasure'.

The Turbo Twin was part of interesting and optimistic times at Royal Enfield. The early 1960s brought a change of ownership of the holding entity, Enfield Cycle Company, and a new sense of confidence in Redditch. Geoff Duke was hired to lead development of a new racing machine, the GP5, and he brought in highly respected two-stroke engineer Herman Meir. The existing design team was producing new, good-looking Interceptors for the US market, a range of pretty 250cc four-stroke unit-construction singles

Although powered by a Villiers-built motor, it was handsomely badged as a Royal Enfield.

for British learners and there was even the promise of an ohc single. There was also talk of a range of all-new step-throughs to take on the Japanese.

And Royal Enfield was going upmarket, with the Turbo Twin not being advertised as the cheap utility machine often associated with motorcycles powered by the proprietary Villiers motors. The large alloy points cover on the Turbo Twin was cast with a raised Enfield Villiers graphic, something not done for any other manufacturer. The TT features several other unique parts, including the top yoke, toolbox and gearbox chain guard cover.

The Villiers 4T engine featured a more angular top end than the preceding 2T and incorporated cylinders with four transfer ports (the 2T had only two) and ported pistons. A Crusader frame was used, while the cycle parts were those of the economy Clipper model, including 17in wheels and 6in brake drums front and rear. Telescopic front forks and Enfield's trademark rear swinging-arm arrangement ensured that this 298lb (135kg) motorcycle could be ridden with great enthusiasm, restricted only by the grounding of the centre stand. Under the tank was a tyre pump, which

was a great idea, but there was also a terrible idea – the choke, activated by a plunger on top of the Villiers carburettor, was impossible to disengage on the move, meaning that the rider was forced to stop once the engine had warmed up.

A low 29in (737mm) seat height was managed without making the Turbo Twin cramped for tall riders. One other thing that was noted by publications in the 1960s was how quiet the bike was on the move, with the silencers designed especially for the 4T.

The suspension was considered firm for the time, but that added to the sporty feel, so it was of no surprise that a Turbo Twin Sports model arrived in 1964. Chrome finish to the tank and mudguards with dropped handlebars marked out the new offering, but as Geoff Duke told prospective buyers, 'Whether your choice is the Standard or Sports model, you'll be thrilled by the exciting new Turbo Twins – genuine value for money that leads the way in the twin-cylinder two-stroke field.' The price was right at £20 more than the existing machine; £215.00 including taxes got you on the road.

This model's futuristic name was an unusual choice, as the word 'turbo' was not yet common in the early 1960s. Just one year prior to its arrival, Chevrolet and Oldsmobile had produced the world's first turbocharged production cars; perhaps this influenced the decision. Alternative opinions consider that the name promotes the silent, super smooth, almost turbine-like power delivery offered by the rubber-mounted Villiers motor. With a nine-bike range on show at Earls Court in 1964 and with Geoff Duke OBE extolling the virtues of the marque to the masses on stand 75, this surely should have been a prosperous time for Royal Enfield.

However, the two-stroke 250 market was about to be completely revolutionized. Yamaha's YDS-2 launched a two-stroke revolution that redefined the 250cc motorcycle in 1962. Before it, people's idea of a quick 250 was something like the Turbo Twin. The YDS-2 was mass-produced, but its design features had grown out of Yamaha's programme to win domestic races and then to enter European GP racing. A figure of 23bhp at 7,500rpm from a 309lb (140kg) motorcycle might be unimpressive today, but fifty-three years ago it was sensational. In February 1963's test, *Motor Cycle* found that it would easily and repeatedly exceed 80mph (129km/h), stirred along with a five-speed gearbox. The racing derivative, the TD1-A, gave a claimed 32bhp at 9,500rpm, and took Yamaha's first Grand Prix win with a 1–2 placing in the 250 class at the 1963 Belgian Grand Prix; Phil Read would take the 250 World Championship for Yamaha the following year.

These factory racers developed Yamaha's Autolube system, which fed oil directly to hotspots and did away with the need to add oil to a two-stroke motor's fuel. It was available on showroom models for 1964, winning Autolube an Award for Excellence from the American Society of Mechanical Engineers. This was an even more valuable addition to the step-through and commuter market, where simplicity of operation mattered to owners who were unlikely to be enthusiasts. After a brief spell as a fine 250 stroker, the Turbo Twin was rendered obsolete almost overnight.

The TT had sold well, with over 700 being made, although Enfield seemed to have hoped for more, as the Villiers manufactured silencers were fitted to Crusaders for years, to the detriment of performance. Other TT parts also found their way on to other models, including the top yoke appearing on the Mk1A Interceptor and the toolbox, complete with a dummy switch left lid, was used on the late Mk1 Interceptors. But once more buying a Royal Enfield 250 meant buying a single-cylinder four-stroke.

ROYAL ENFIELD TURBO TWIN SPORT SPECIFICATION

Engine
Type: Villiers 249cc Mk 4T two-stroke twin
Carburettor: Villiers S25 plunger type
Fuel capacity: 3½gal (16ltr)

Transmission
Gearbox: Villiers four-speed

Electrics
Type: Lucas 6V

Dimensions
Weight: 298lb (135kg)
Ground clearance: 5½in (140mm)

Performance
Top speed: 75mph (121km/h)/standing ¼-mile 21.6sec
Fuel consumption: 96mpg @ 30mph/52mpg @ 60mph (2.95ltr/100km @ 48km/h/5.44ltr/100km @ 97km/h)

GEOFF DUKE AND THE FINAL FLING: THE CONTINENTAL GT

Geoff Duke was one of the world's first motorcycling superstars, making his racing debut in the 1948 Junior Isle of Man Grand Prix with Norton. Although a split oil tank led to engine failure, causing him to withdraw from the race by the end of the third lap, he was already leading. His first victory came in the 350 race at Haddenham Airfield in 1949, soon followed by wins in the Senior Manx Grand Prix and the Senior Clubman's TT later that year. Duke significantly improved the image of motorcycling and motorcyclists and is credited with developing the one-piece race suit. Charismatic, well-spoken and impeccably presented, he was voted Sportsman of the Year in 1951 – an unprecedented feat for a motorcycle racer – and awarded an OBE in 1953. During his short career, ended prematurely with a crash in a Cooper Formula 1 car in Sweden in 1961, his prowess was second to none. He secured six world championships and six Isle of Man TT wins.

His race record was even more impressive than the championship wins. With thirty-three wins from sixty-six Grand Prix starts, he finished on the podium a further seventeen times. In 1955, he became the first rider to lap the Isle of Man TT course at 100mph (161km/h), although this was later downgraded to 99.97mph (160.5km/h). Duke's smooth riding style was declared by Stanley Woods, the renowned Irish racer, as like 'water flowing from a tap'.

Geoff Duke joined Royal Enfield in 1964, his brief to revitalize the company's image and sales alongside development of the GP5 250cc programme, which is detailed in Chapter 9. One of the first signs of this change of direction was the Continental GT, a fine example of a manufacturer sticking its head above the parapet to see what the market wanted rather than telling it what it could have. Unlike the Airflow Crusader, the Airflow fairing available for the Continental GT was pure grand-prix racer and, intriguingly, the fibreglass tank, rear sets and seat from the 250 GT would fit straight on to the 750 Interceptor. Available from 1965, this 21bhp variant of the Crusader had a five-speed gearbox (which was also an option on the Crusader), clip-on handlebars and rear-set footrests.

The stunning looks of the Continental GT contrasted with its progenitor, the Super Five, which was the first British motorcycle to boast a five-speed gearbox and for some reason was painted in what looked like grey primer.

The GT 250 really hit the nail on the head, a perfect sporting 250 for those with L-plates. BONHAMS

The GT 250 was especially
handsome with the
optional sports fairing.
BONHAMS

Even as standard, the GT
came with a screen and
clip-on handlebars.

Offered for only two model seasons (1962 and 1963), featuring Enfield's own short leading-link front forks, it proved too different, too much too soon, and too expensive.

The Super Five was not only first with the five-speed gearbox, but that was not the only departure from normal practice. The complex leading-link forks might have improved handling, but they looked odd and added to costs even if the front mudguard was fixed to the forks instead of the wheel, reducing unsprung weight. Deep valences on the front mudguard – so deep that they could display the registration number on their sides – kept road grime off the rider, as did the side panel cum rear mudguard. An extra large nacelle without pilot lights enclosed the entire top of the forks, adding to the rather boxy and stumpy styling. Stylish and elegant is was not, but it was pricey at about 30 per cent more than BSA's C15.

On top of this, the five-speed gearbox was fragile and prone to false neutral issues that Albion, which built Enfield's gearboxes, never resolved. In truth, there just wasn't enough room in the unit-construction crankcase for a sufficiently beefy five speeds and many were retrospectively converted to four speeds. Even so, this was the starting point for the much better looking and better loved Continental GT, which everyone was sure would be a hit single. The only problem was telling people how good it was.

Royal Enfield was struggling to compete with Honda's big budget advertising and racing programmes. To fight back, Royal Enfield hired famous racer John 'Moon Eyes' Cooper to join Duke on a 24-hour sprint in a team of five riders to dash from John O'Groats to Land's End on Wednesday, 11 November 1964. On the way, they planned a stop at Oulton Park for Duke to ride several laps – cancelled due to ice on the track – and also a stop at Silverstone. Here, Cooper turned in several laps at an average of 70.29mph (113.12km/h), with a fastest lap of 73mph (117.5km/h). The team of riders thrashed the new Continental GT from John O'Groats to Land's End in a little over twenty-two hours, ensuring that the new Royal Enfield 250 was well and truly launched in a blaze of positive publicity. Enfield could only afford much smaller advertisements than Honda's full-page spreads, but still it was enough to point out that this was Britain's fastest 250 and positively dripping with goodies, a true café racer for the L-plate generation.

Thus the Continental GT became the dream motorcycle of every learner rider of the mid-1960s and was seen as the saviour of an ailing Royal Enfield company suffering the onslaughts of the massed hordes of Japanese and Italian lightweights. The bright red fibreglass tank, polychrome silver frame, grey handlebar grips, hump-backed, two-tone seat and the natty fly screen led to arguably one of the prettiest production motorcycles of the day, especially with the optional full fairing. A handful were also made with cross-braced motocross style handlebars for the US market in 1967, but 1967 was also the end of the road for the Redditch factory and its single-cylinder motorcycles. All that was left was the big twins and the works at Bradford-on-Avon.

ROYAL ENFIELD CONTINENTAL GT SPECIFICATION

Engine
Type: air-cooled single-cylinder four-stroke
Bore × stroke: 70 × 64.5mm
Capacity: 248cc
Valves: overhead, pushrod activated
Ignition: battery and coil
Max. power: 21bhp at 7,500rpm
Fuel system: single Amal Concentric carburettor

Transmission
Type: five-speed

Suspension
Front: telescopic forks
Rear: twin shocks

Brakes
Front: drum
Rear: drum

Dimensions
Weight: 330lb (150kg)

Performance
Top speed: 80mph (129km/h)

8

THE BIG TWINS

A nice and unmolested Royal Enfield 500 twin. JACKYP

As we have seen, Britain's trade deficit had been growing since the mid-1930s and World War II virtually brought export sales to an end, while the UK imported everything from food to fighter aircraft. By the end of the war, Britain had lost two-thirds of its export markets and was having to rely upon American loans as well as repaying the wartime lease-lend arrangements. With the Empire fading fast there was really only one market to look toward – the United States itself. And with steel only available to businesses that exported much of their production, the UK Government had one message to manufacturers and that was to export or die.

The desires of the post-war US road rider were pretty straightforward: big capacity four-stroke twins in a package that didn't weigh too much. Great styling and gleaming alloy to look sharp at the stoplights – and the ability to leave those stoplights in a hurry. Those at Harley-Davidson thought they understood this, but their machines weighed far too much, leading to riders removing much of the tinware and shortening the rear mudguard, a practice known as bobbing – the term taken from horse racing and docked tails – and so creating bobber motorcycles.

The real heartthrob of US riders was the Triumph Speed Twin, a machine that became the vertical twin template for the entire British motorcycle industry. Edward Turner first considered the idea at Ariel, as half of his Square Four. When Ariel bought Triumph in 1935 Turner embarked on creating the Speed Twin, which first appeared in 1937. There had been vertical twins before, but Turner's was lighter and narrower than even the single-cylinder Tiger 90, whose cycle parts it shared. The Speed Twin proved an enormous success for Triumph, setting it on the road to prosperity. Performance proved exemplary for a road-going 500: a top speed of around 85mph (137km/h) with the Tiger 100 sports version and the potential to reach the magic ton.

The twin-cylinder engine was a long-stroke 498cc (63 × 80mm bore and stroke), which, with an Amal 276/132¹⁵⁄₁₆in (24mm) carburettor, a Lucas Magdyno and a 7:1 compression ratio, gave 26bhp at 6,000rpm. There was a separate oil tank and a four-speed gearbox: dry sump and pre-unit construction. A Girder front fork and a sprung saddle provided the suspension, with drum brakes in both the 20in front wheel and 19in rear. Total weight was 355lb (161kg).

On the night of 14 November 1940, the majority of the city centre of Coventry was destroyed by German bombs and the Triumph factory (which was working on an order of thousands of military specification 5Ts) was completely wiped out, and all of Triumph's technical records, drawings and designs were destroyed. After the war Triumph's new factory at Meriden pretty much had to revisit the Speed Twin from scratch, but a redeveloped Speed Twin went on sale in 1946 with telescopic forks and optional sprung hub rear suspension. It was another instant hit, developed by Edward Turner – a huge fan of the United States where he spent much time – along with his stylist and personal assistant, Jack Wickes. Wickes was head of Triumph's Design Department and developed the flowing lines of the classic Triumph profile, often introduced by Turner as 'my pencil'.

The late 1960s Triumph Bonneville was probably their finest hour, understanding US riders' desires to a tee. Chasing the same market, the Laverda 650/750, based upon Honda's 305cc Hawk, was a good first try, as was Honda's CB450, although this proved Laverda right and that selling 444cc motorcycles with 750 performance was one thing: allowing your customers to boast that they had an actual 750 was quite another. It was a lesson that Royal Enfield would be quick to learn.

ROYAL ENFIELD'S FIRST TWIN

The 500 Twin was the first post-war twin-cylinder motorcycle to be built by Royal Enfield and was its first vertical parallel twin. Almost everything apart from the engine was shared with the Bullet, so the chassis featured telescopic front forks, twin rear shock absorbers and Royal Enfield's original swinging arm. Thus, along with the 350 Bullet, the 500 Twin was the first production motorcycle with a true swinging-arm rear suspension. Launched in 1948 and despite the cutting-edge chassis, the Royal Enfield's twin-cylinder motor looked as if it was simply playing catch-up with the Speed Twin and BSA's very similar A7 that was launched alongside the Triumph in 1946 (Triumph was owned by BSA at the time). At least Royal Enfield was quicker off the mark than Norton, with its plunger-framed twin-cylinder Dominator Model 7 going on sale in mid-1949 and becoming a template for Norton twins for the next thirty years.

Despite Royal Enfield's swinging-arm frame and telescopic fork being bang up to date, the motor largely followed orthodox lines. Like its rivals, the crank was a 360-degree item to allow a single carburettor to be fitted, the same Amal fitted to the Speed Twin. However, use of separate barrels and cylinder heads was unusual, as well as incorporation of the oil tank within the crankcase – a feature inherited from the Redditch firm's singles – and dynamically balanced nodular iron crankshaft. Largely the work of Bullet designer Ted Pardoe rather than Tony Wilson-Jones, the 64 × 77mm bore and stroke mimicked the pre-war Model S 250 and was notably short stroke compared to the Speed Twin. Alloy domed pistons had a modest 6.5:1 compression ratio, reflecting the quality of available fuel, although higher compression items were an option. The separate barrels were interchangeable with deep spigots into the crankcase, as on the Bullet. An oil filter was under a cover that looked like the Bullet's oil

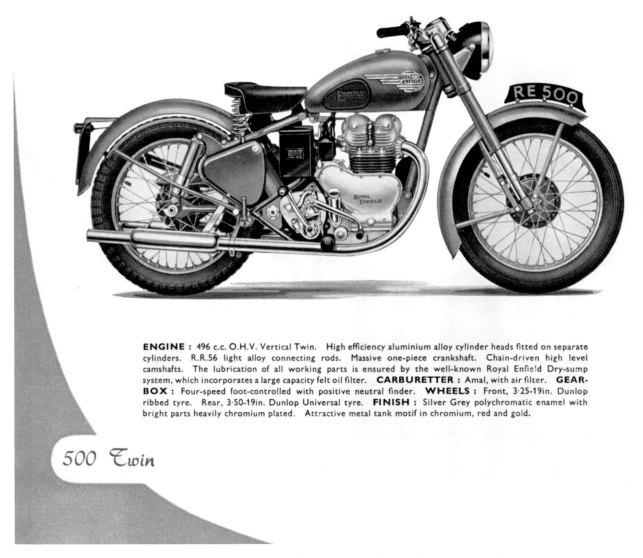

ENGINE : 496 c.c. O.H.V. Vertical Twin. High efficiency aluminium alloy cylinder heads fitted on separate cylinders. R.R.56 light alloy connecting rods. Massive one-piece crankshaft. Chain-driven high level camshafts. The lubrication of all working parts is ensured by the well-known Royal Enfield Dry-sump system, which incorporates a large capacity felt oil filter. **CARBURETTER :** Amal, with air filter. **GEAR-BOX :** Four-speed foot-controlled with positive neutral finder. **WHEELS :** Front, 3·25-19in. Dunlop ribbed tyre. Rear, 3·50-19in. Dunlop Universal tyre. **FINISH :** Silver Grey polychromatic enamel with bright parts heavily chromium plated. Attractive metal tank motif in chromium, red and gold.

500 Twin

A side view makes it easy to understand how the 500 Twins are often mistaken for Bullets.

filler. The drive side had a single row ball-race bearing for the hollow crank matched by a roller bearing on the timing side. A central flywheel and balance rather than a third bearing would lead to issues with the crank whipping, but generally this was a sturdy piece of work. Primary chain drive was to a bolted-on Albion gearbox, again mimicking the Bullet.

It was simply marketed as the '500 Twin' and, with most non-engine parts shared with the Bullet, it was not an imposing motorcycle. Its power of 25bhp at 5,500rpm was down on the Speed Twin, but at 390lb (177kg) it was

10 per cent heavier. It was also expensive, especially compared to BSA's equivalent A7. Something had to change. For 1950, that amounted to a polished alloy facia for the Smith's speedometer, but 1951 brought die-cast crankcases and a corresponding drop in weight. This required expensive new tooling, explaining why it would be 1955 before the cylinder heads were also die-cast alloy. Between those years a dual seat option was offered and revised oil feed, including external lines to the cylinder heads addressing oil leak issues. The famous die-cast alloy handlebar casquette also arrived.

The ex-works, Jack Stocker, 1951 ISDT Gold Medal-winning, 1951 Royal Enfield 495cc Twin. BONHAMS

A dual front brake, albeit still just a 6in item, arrived in 1955, along with a 7in (rather than 6in) rear drum, finally addressing the poor stopping. A Magdyno was now standard behind a new gearbox cover, although it would be 1957 before there was a crank-mounted alternator. By now, compression was up to 7.25:1, with a new Amal 376 carburettor, albeit without an enlarged bore. Finally there was a Speed Twin-matching 27bhp at 6,000rpm, but the slow pace of development reflected just how modest a concern Royal Enfield was compared to rivals BSA and Triumph. Or it may have been its focus on the 692cc Meteor 700 that had been launched in 1952 to become Britain's biggest twin.

METEOR MINOR

The Meteor 700 had been launched with an especially robust frame suitable for fast sidecar journeys; the London Earls Court Motorcycle Show bike was fitted with a Watsonian sidecar. In a fit of rationalization, the 1957 500 Twin received

the full loop Meteor frame and in 1958 was overhauled and relaunched as the Meteor Minor. The pre-war 64 × 77mm bore and stroke architecture was updated with replaceable big-end shells and to mimic the new unit 250 singles at 70 × 64.5mm, a clear attempt to increase power. The carburettor was a larger 1¹/₁₆in (27mm) Amal 376 Monobloc, compression jumped to 8:1 and 30bhp arrived at 6,250rpm. The smaller 17in wheels were also from the 250s, but with a 6in full-width dual brake at the front and a 7in single at the rear. Helped by a two into one exhaust system, weight was down 20lb (9kg), which, with the 10 per cent power boost, put 90mph (145km/h) within reach. A deluxe model upgraded the specification to a 7in front brake, dual seat and better protection from grime with deeper mudguards and a fully enclosed chain, the latter necessitating a quickly detachable rear wheel. The Airflow fairing was an option, which gifted the standard model the 7in front brake.

Inevitably, even this was not enough and the Meteor Minor Sports followed in 1960, with hot cams and even higher compression pistons. Styling mimicked the range-topping

Constellation 700, and 33bhp at a heady 6,500rpm allowed Royal Enfield to claim that this was 'a 500 that handles like a 250 … a luxury sports machine capable of speeds in the region of 95–100mph'.

The Meteor Minor was no longer the gentleman's carriage of old. Gone was the pleasant, vibration-free tourer and in its place a rev-hungry rider rattler had arrived. This was an acceptable trade-off if you were a young man in a hurry, but less so for a family man. The fact that the sidecar specification – revised trail and gear ratios, firmer springing and a steering damper – was now a no-cost option hinted at the malaise.

The Citroën 2CV had been the start of a post-war pursuit of cheap four-wheeled family transport followed by arguably its greatest proponent, Fiat's 500 Nuova in 1957. BMC

(British Motor Corporation) launched the Mini in April 1959 at an on the road price of £537. A Meteor Minor Sport was £270, plus a family man would want a sidecar; or, if he wanted a big sidecar, the Constellation 700. Of course, what he did was sign up for hire purchase and buy the Mini, leaving the big motorcycle market to the young speed freaks, especially in the USA. Suddenly big motorcycles were about American buyers not because they were being urged by government to export, but because the traditional sidecar market was about to die. After cars and Scotch whisky, motorcycles were the UK's biggest export in an age of economic turmoil and a horrific balance of payments deficit that would lead to sterling's 1967 devaluation.

Into this perfect storm rode the Japanese. How few realized that the end of the British motorcycle industry was barely a decade away, with the factories still proudly boasting of magnificent profits and much admired motorcycles, both reported on in the press with deserved admiration. This hubris meant that the British saw the arrival of Japanese products especially as a chance to expand markets in general and to allow the British to focus on high profit margins rather than quantity. But the UK motorcycle market had already peaked in 1959 and the British motorcycle factories turned once again to the US market to maintain sales and profitability. Yet Honda was already one step ahead of them, as JoMo (Johnson Motors), one of Triumph's brace of US distributors, discovered.

Honda sales manager Hirobumi Nakamura agreed to meet the JoMo team, rather than the Vice President they had invited. After introductions and small talk JoMo team leader Bill Johnson asked how many motorcycles Honda expected to sell in the USA. 'Five thousand,' was the confident reply. At the time, JoMo was selling some 2,500 motorcycles a year in its nineteen-state western territories, so, not unreasonably, Johnson responded that 5,000 a year 'was a lot of motorcycles'.

'No, 5,000 motorcycles a month,' came the reply. But a flabbergasted Johnson, like his British counterparts, soon got over his shock and came to the view that this would just grow the market, ultimately to the benefit of heavyweights such as the big Triumph and Harley-Davidson twins. Certainly there was no attempt to undermine or even compete with Honda through much of the 1960s, let alone stop the company recruiting US dealers. Although it was against anti-trust laws to insist that US dealers only stocked one marque, in practice it happened with distributors such as JoMo turning a blind eye if a dealer also stocked a small volume brand such as Ducati or Jawa, allowing them to claim adherence to the letter of the law, if not the spirit. And so Honda was allowed a bridgehead alongside the tiny European factories. Except that Honda was soon flooding the showrooms.

The irony was that Honda had learnt from Triumph, copying Triumph's showroom layouts, warranties and even its marketing strategy. Who can forget Honda encouraging everybody to take up motorcycling with its 'You Meet The Nicest People on a Honda' campaign? Yet a decade earlier, US Triumph dealers had been specifically promised by Triumph that prospective buyers meant 'non-riders; the young men and women in school, the professional man, the businessman, the bank president, the church minister, the commuter, the sportsman, the serviceman … just to name a few'. The problem was that Honda was out to get those buyers too and was armed with resources and production capacities that BSA – indeed everybody else – could only dream of. Yet, for now at least, even the Americans, to use one of their best-known phrases, had yet to 'wake up and smell the coffee'. Royal Enfield, as a bit player to the mighty BSA-Triumph productions, could but hang on to their coat tails and hope for the best.

Ironically, the American Triumph importers were so impressed with the number of machines that Honda's new dealers were selling – many of them new to motorcycles – that exclusively Triumph franchises were torn up and new free for all contracts awarded, often to these new-wave Japanese dealers. Initially, this brought a flood of orders, as the Honda dealers had the footfall from the smaller Hondas that quickly fed into sales for bigger British bikes. The scheme worked well until the CB450 Honda arrived and even then buyers often stuck to British bikes, preferring to show off a 650 or a Royal Enfield 700 rather than a 450 that was just as quick. But Turner's belief that Honda was decades away from being able to build a 'big bike' should have been challenged at this stage, rather than await the rumour of a new 750. Even so, Honda's bridgehead into America was now unassailable.

GO BIG OR GO HOME – THE METEOR 700

Going back less than a decade, to the 1952 Earls Court Motorcycle Show, reveals how quickly the old certainties had faded. The Meteor 700 was the biggest new kid on the block, a throwback to the big pre-war V-twins in spirit, if not in layout. Shown with a sidecar, it was naturally available with optional sidecar front forks and gearing. As a torquey solo it would be marketed as the Indian Trailblazer in the USA, part of a range of Indian badged Royal Enfield twins, which, as we shall see, were offered in America.

Ted Pardoe was a huge fan of modular concepts, keeping the number of parts across the entire Royal Enfield range to a minimum. The bore and stroke of the separate iron barrels thus copied the 350 Bullet's 70 × 90mm and the crankcase was from the 500 Twin, the strength and deep cylinder spigots allowing Royal Enfield to leap BSA and Triumph's 650s in a single bound. Con rods were still RR56

A 1960 Meteor Minor Sport. BONHAMS

Royal Enfield again choosing colourful advertising and emphasizing the compact nature of its motorcycles.
A HERL INC

A 1953 693cc Meteor. BONHAMS

aluminium alloy, but replaceable shell bearings were used from the start. Alloy cylinder heads aided cooling and, like the barrels, were separate castings; 36bhp was claimed at 6,000rpm, an extra clutch plate being an upgrade from the 500 Twin. Initially, coil ignition was fitted, but, like its smaller cousins, the Meteor got a Magdyno in 1955. Indeed, upgrades tended to come across the range, with updates to the 500 Twin and its successors as well as those applied to the Bullet being used to improve the Meteor. Since these developments have already been detailed when dealing with the Bullet and 500 Twin they will not be repeated here.

The Meteor's cycle parts were mostly shared with the 500 Twin range, with a larger 4gal (18ltr) fuel tank. The frame's beefy proportions, especially the swinging arm, again hinted at the expectation of sidecar fitment. Tester Brian Crow spent weeks riding on the cobbles at MIRA testing alternative rear shock absorbers before rejecting in-house units for items from Armstrong in Yorkshire. These were firmer in sidecar specification, with the forks

also modified and fitted with a steering damper. All the gear ratios were different to the solo specification. Yet the dual 6in front brakes and 7in rear were marginal at best on a solo, while the Albion gearbox became troublesome with a sidecar fitted. Optional panniers were good quality, but inevitably added yet more weight. The prototype was entered into the British ISDT test in Wales in May 1952 with long-time factory tester 'Jolly Jack' Stocker, his talent perhaps proven by the fact none of the Meteor's shortcomings were addressed before it went on sale.

But while the Meteor's 692cc capacity leapfrogged the competition, the 405lb (184kg) Meteor was no fire-breathing sportster. Rather, it was an echo of the sidecar lugging V-twins of old and was described by road tester Bob Currie as 'a rather woolly animal intended primarily for sidecar haulage'. In other words a mammoth rather than a sabre-toothed tiger. Even though in the next incarnation, the 1955 40bhp Super Meteor introduced in 1955, it succeeded in travelling at the magic ton, somehow road testers still did not explode with incandescent enthusiasm.

The big change with the Super Meteor was the switch from barrel spigots sitting in the crankcase mouth to dowels. This, with a shuffle of the pushrod tubes, allowed bigger gaskets to try to stem the perennial oil leaks. These would not be helped by increased compression (7.25:1), a doubling of the oil-flow rate and better gas flow by adopting changes from the Bullet. The gearbox was modified to allow the gear-shift lever to be concentric with the kick-start. A Lucas alternator and Amal Monobloc carburettor were also upgrades. The frame was finally all-welded, apart from a lug at the steering head, and various rubber parts were added to address vibration damaging components.

In 1957, Burgess silencers were introduced, also as per the Bullet, and the following year the Airflow option. Modified engines, incorporating electric starts, were also produced by the factory for the Berkeley B95 and B105 car models during 1959 and 1960. There were Silentbloc swinging-arm bushes in 1961 rather than bronze bushes, partly to address vibration but at the expense of handling. As previously discussed, by this time sales of motorcycles aimed at sidecar enthusiasts were in serious decline and by 1963 the Meteor name was gone, superseded by the Constellation and Interceptor aimed straight at the US performance enthusiast.

A Super Meteor, still 693cc, from 1959. BONHAMS

The Constellation might have still been 693cc, but it was more highly tuned, though with unhappy consequences. This is a 1960 model. BONHAMS

1959 ROYAL ENFIELD CONSTELLATION

As we have seen, the launch of the Mini in April 1959 at an on the road price of £537 killed the sidecar market, when a typical big British twin with a family-sized Watsonian bolted on would cost the best part of £400. Readily available hire purchase did the rest and the car people were not going to stop there. Ford's answer was the new Anglia 105 at £610 and, after reputedly buying a Mini and deciding that its comparatively complex front-wheel drive meant Ford could build a much bigger car for the same money, the company launched the Ford (Consul) Cortina in October 1962. This two-door saloon was a bargain, the base model retailing for a mere £639 compared with the £675 retail price of the Morris 1100.

The stylish Cortina was a proper five-seater with a heater that would become a best seller and turn sidecar outfits into a niche interest. Suddenly the British factories had to find another market for their big twins, so they looked to Triumph's success in the USA as an exemplar. Something eye-catching, stylish and as fast as possible for traffic-light credibility was required, as well as something to remind American citizens of the space race; 1958 was the year in which the USA launched its own satellite, Explorer I, and created the National Aeronautics and Space Administration (NASA). Constellation was a timely reminder that the British could be counted upon to support its cousins over the Atlantic. Now please buy our new motorcycle …

The Constellation had a refreshed crankcase design, the old dies used for the 500 Twin and Meteors having

Rechroming fuel tanks can be problematic, so this 1961 model was restored with just grey paint. BONHAMS

A 1962 Constellation, again painted rather than rechromed. BONHAMS

worn out. This gave the designers the chance to fit the camshafts higher and make the pushrods shorter, even though the Constellation had a long-stroke engine. The redesign also allowed the camshafts to be removed and replaced through access holes in the primary side without splitting the cases.

The barrels, separate as on Enfield's previous parallel twins, were so deeply set in the crankcase that they were almost oil-cooled: or heated – with a small 4pt (2.3ltr) oil tank within the crankcase Royal Enfield's unique architecture might have been tidier and freer of unnecessary oil lines compared to a separate oil tank below the seat, but with the increased power the Constellation ran very hot. The dynamically balanced crankshaft was beefed up, there were special Nimonic valves, mimicking those fitted to BSA's Gold Star, and a single $^{13}/_{16}$in (30mm) Amal TT racing carburettor. Electrics were powered by an alternator with a Lucas competition magneto with a manual advance/retard.

Unusual for the time was the Enfield's ignition system. Instead of the usual magneto was a coil ignition system fed by a 6V battery charged by a DC generator. Contact breaker points were mounted inside a distributor driven off the generator.

In typical Enfield fashion, the semi-unit four-speed Albion gearbox was bolted to the back of the engine. The Albion unit had a reputation as being very agricultural, but very, very, strong. Sadly, the same was not true of Enfield's notorious 'scissor' clutch, which was marginal on the Super Meteor.

The frame, front and rear suspension and cycle parts followed the same year's Bullet single surprisingly closely and, although strengthened, the engine mounts would prove inadequate. This, combined with the bolted-up nature of the motor, with separate cylinders and heads, meant that the chassis lacked rigidity compared to the competition. It also left those who rode their machines hard discovering that the engine would work loose in the frame.

The 'Big Three' British factories were already in something of a power race by the late 1950s, with BSA and Triumph's flagship models, the Super Rocket and Tiger 110, making 46 and 42bhp respectively. Norton's 49bhp 650SS was waiting in the wings, as was Triumph's 46bhp Bonneville. So Royal Enfield needed a power boost from the 700 engine when the Constellation arrived for the

1958 season. Compared to the Super Meteor, compression went from 7.25:1 to 8.5:1, and it had hotter cams, a siamezed exhaust system and a claimed 'over 50bhp' at 6,250rpm. Unfortunately, the engine also produced the kind of vibration you might expect from a big 360-degree parallel twin, although thanks to the balanced crankshaft the Constellation was better than most.

Fondly known as the Connie, Royal Enfield's Constellation had an impressive turn of speed; the claimed 110mph (177km/h) potential was actually comfortably bettered when tested by *Motor Cycling*. Averaging 80mph (129km/h) and an impressive 51mpg (5.6ltr/100km) on a trip to Belgium, the icing on the cake was a genuine 115mph (185km/h) top speed. Sadly, the machine suffered from oil leaks and the scissor clutch was prone to slipping.

For 1960, a pair of $^{13}/_{16}$in (30mm) Amal Monobloc carburettors replaced the racing TT carb. The tight fit behind the engine left no room for the right-side carburettor's float bowl, so both were fed from a single float bowl on the left side. Forward pointing 'ears' were added to the side panels at the same time. As was the fashion at the time, the Constellation got some body panels around the rear wheel for 1961 and a new, flatter dual seat.

The final iteration of the Constellation was in 1963. With production of the replacement Interceptor in full flow, the Constellation was repositioned as a sidecar tug, with the Super Meteor-spec 7.25:1 compression 40bhp engine, coil ignition, big mudguards, steering damper and revised 'sidecar' fork moving the front axle farther forward. But by that time the sidecar market was dead and the Constellation died with it. It was a sad example of a small-scale factory trying to leapfrog the big boys and discovering that it didn't have the resources to develop fully a cutting-edge product, let alone deal with the consequences when things went wrong. The Constellation was a nightmare for Royal Enfield and for those who bought one: the bills could get as big as a full rebuild, including new crankcases. No wonder the Constellation name was dropped when Royal Enfield comprehensively overhauled its big twin.

So the big news from Enfield in 1962 was a new model with one more stretch for the twin. Bore increased 1mm to 71, while the stroke grew 3mm to 93mm for a capacity of 736cc. The Interceptor would remain in production in various forms until Royal Enfield's final demise around 1970.

1959 ROYAL ENFIELD CONSTELLATION SPECIFICATION

Engine
Type: 693cc air-cooled ohv parallel twin
Bore and stroke: 70mm × 90mm
Compression ratio: 8.5:1, 51hp @ 6,250rpm (claimed)
Carburettor: single 1³/₁₆in Amal 10TT9
Fuel capacity: 5gal (18.9ltr)/51mpg (5.6ltr/100km) (period test)

Transmission
Gearbox: four-speed with neutral finder, chain final drive

Electrics
Type: 6V, magneto ignition

Suspension
Front: telescopic fork
Rear: dual shocks with adjustable preload
Tyres: 3.25 × 19in front, 3.50 × 19in rear

Brakes
Front: 6in double-sided SLS drum
Rear: 7in SLS drum

Dimensions
Frame: single down-tube cradle frame
Wheelbase: 54in (1,372mm)
Weight (dry): 403lb (183kg)
Seat height: 31in (787mm)

Performance
Top speed: 115mph (185km/h) (period test)

INTERCEPTOR

The first Interceptor was not the heavily revised Constellation of 1963, but rather a limited run of Constellation-based specials for the US market in 1961, sold as the 700 Interceptor. Noting the success of BSA's Spitfire Scrambler – introduced in 1957 at the request of BSA's West Coast distributor, Hap Alzina – it was squarely aimed at beating the dominant Triumph twins in desert racing. Very much a competition model, BSA quickly adopted the style across its North

American range and Royal Enfield decided to follow suit. So the Interceptor 700 was equipped for off-road enduro-style events – or rather not, as it lacked road equipment and without the history of US competition success that Triumph and BSA had in the USA the 700 stuck to showroom floors. Eventually most of the 160-odd Interceptor 700s were retrofitted by dealers with aftermarket horns, mirrors and lights and sold for road use.

And then, in late 1962, Royal Enfield bored and stroked the Constellation's engine to 736cc to launch the 750 Interceptor. Brockhouse Engineering of West Bromwich, close to many of the British motorcycle factories including Royal Enfield, acted as US importer for most of them. But in 1959 Norton jumped ship to the New Jersey-based Berliner Corporation, launching the first British 750, the new Norton Atlas 750, again in 1962. Brockhouse wanted revenge and a competing 750, and only Royal Enfield was able to oblige at short notice. So, like the Norton, the Interceptor 750 was offered stateside before becoming available in the UK.

There were two variants of the first Interceptor 750 for the US market: one with a polished alloy instrument nacelle rather than black paint; and a polished alloy wing nut for the steering damper, rather than a black round knob. The MkI (Series 1 in the UK) Interceptors that were sold outside the USA had bigger fuel tanks, twin-sided 6in front brakes and shorter swinging arms and wheelbase. They also had 8:1 compression rather than the 8.5:1 of the US models.

Enfield dynamically balanced its big twin engines, reducing vibration compared to large displacement bikes made by competitors, who used static balancing. The long-stroke design produced abundant torque from low revs, making the bikes very tractable and capable of impressive acceleration. On the downside, the separate barrels and heads meant that the engines tended to flex, which, combined with poor crankcase venting, led to the bikes having a reputation for leaking oil and thus the nickname 'Royal Oilfield'. Having said that, *The Motor Cycle* reported on the remarkable oil tightness of their example, suggesting a machine built especially for the press, something that was common practice at BSA.

The Interceptor was upgraded in 1964 with a second fuel tap, float bowls on both Amal Monoblocs, magnetic instruments, Girling rear shock absorbers, an auto-advance magneto, hotter 'R' (Supersport) camshafts, and one less tooth on the gearbox sprocket for better acceleration. In the USA the 1964 model was known as the TT Interceptor. The single carburettor Custom with standard camshaft was added

This handsome Series I Interceptor was the first Royal Enfield 750. BONHAMS

Rechroming fuel tanks may be difficult/expensive, but this 1965 Interceptor shows that it's worth it. BONHAMS

in 1965 and the 1966 GT with twin carburettors and sport cams meant that there were three MkI models available that year. There were 979 MkIs produced between 1962 and 1966.

The Interceptor MkIa was introduced in late 1966. Produced at new facilities in Bradford-on-Avon, it featured twin Amal concentric carburettors, coil ignition and better engine breathing. Two models differing only in cosmetic aspects were offered in the USA: the Road Scrambler TT7 with upswept pipes, chrome tank and exposed chrome shock springs; and the Road Racer GP7 with low exhausts, a painted tank and shrouded shocks, looking more like the old MkI. The 1962 and 1963 Series I had twin ¹³⁄₁₆in (30mm) Amal Monoblocs sharing one float bowl, a Lucas K2F manual-advance magneto, a 6V alternator and the four-speed Albion gearbox with a neutral finder. The fuel tank had a single tap with no reserve position, while a Smiths chronometric speedometer and tachometer were standard.

Royal Enfield produced its final UK-built twin, the Interceptor Series 2 (aka the MkII) from 1968 to 1970. The engine was comprehensively redesigned by Reg Thomas, who was principally responsible for the original Interceptor and unit singles. By now, the Redditch factory was gone and strictly speaking so had the Enfield Cycle Company, its ownership passing to Denis Poore's Norton-Villiers, later Norton-Villiers Triumph (NVT), in turn owned by Manganese Bronze.

Royal Enfield motorcycles were now exclusively the product of Enfield Precision Engineers based at Bradford-on-Avon, so that it became debatable who owned the Royal Enfield name. This was further complicated by E. & H.P. Smith having sold the Royal Enfield spares business to Velocette, who had been building frames for the twins. In practice, Enfield Precision Engineers simply gave up on motorcycles to focus on Ministry of Defence work and had no interest in the trademark, and nor did E. & H.P. Smith. It would be 2001 before Enfield India finally resolved the issue.

Reg Thomas's redesign of the Series 2 Interceptor featured a new crankcase with a wet sump and the contact points were relocated in the timing cover. Norton forks and front brake were still used. The Series 2 bikes leaked less oil than the earlier versions, but were heavier and slower. The factory had plans for an 800cc Interceptor Mk3 successor, but never put it into production, although prototypes were made and road-tested. There is more on this in a later chapter from factory development rider Richard Stevens.

The Royal Enfield Interceptor could reasonably claim to be one of the first superbikes of the 1960s. When a MkI ran a 13.8sec quarter-mile, *Cycle World* proclaimed it the quickest stock production bike they had ever tested. In addition, a bike powered by two Royal Enfield Interceptor engines was the first non-streamlined motorcycle to exceed 200mph

This Series 2 Interceptor is a US model, the new tank reminiscent of the Continental GT. BONHAMS

This bike, powered by two Royal Enfield Interceptor engines, was the first non-streamlined motorcycle to exceed 200mph (322km/h), hitting 203.16mph (326.9km/h) at Bonneville in 1970.

(322km/h), hitting 203.16mph (326.9km/h) at Bonneville in 1970. It was a glorious swansong.

THE OTHER INDIAN ENFIELDS – COMPETING WITH HARLEY-DAVIDSON IN THE USA

The big British twins might have been loved in the USA but none of these motorcycles could offer what a US buyer really wanted – an American name on the fuel tank. The head of Honda UK once told me that sales dropped for a fortnight every time *Bridge on the River Kwai* was shown on TV, so the Japanese had an even bigger struggle. But motorcycle buyers knew that Harley-Davidsons were slow and heavy, with poor brakes even by Royal Enfield's standards, yet they were made in the United States of America. What else could a patriot buy?

There had once been the option of buying from TT winners Indian, of course. Built in Springfield – chosen as a home town by the Simpson's creator because it is such a common US place name – Indian thought it was smart in World War I to focus on supplying its dealers rather than the military. However, in the long run, Harley's decision to

do the opposite proved the right one. Yet the Indian name still had resonance, as well as a certain cool that Harley did not. However, when the outlaw One Percenters and Hell's Angels adopted the marque, not everybody wanted to ride a motorcycle with those associations and Indian motorcycles of Springfield were bankrupted in 1953.

If only someone could relaunch Indian, surely they would clean up and, as most people know, that person was Floyd Clymer. Everyone seems to remember that Clymer was caught up in dubious practices pursuing the Great American Dream and spent time in prison, although the tale is controversial, with a number of forces at work. This is not a story of a cowboy and Indians: Clymer was dealing in bikes from the age of twelve, became a member of the famous Harley Wrecking Crew race team and went on to be publisher of his eponymous motorcycle manuals and *Cycle* magazine. None of this was enough for Clymer. He was determined to revive Indian.

His first attempt to buy Indian came shortly after the Springfield factory closed in 1953, but marque owner Brockhouse Engineering in England turned him down, preferring to sell rebadged Royal Enfields as Indians in the USA.

Thus Brockhouse imported the Indian Fire Arrow 250 based on the Royal Enfield Clipper, the 150 Lance (Ensign), Woodsman and Westerner (Bullet), Tomahawk (500 Twin) and Trailblazer (Meteor/Super Meteor). These were followed by the Chief, based on the Constellation, with 16in wheels and available in full police trim. The changes were cosmetic and, apart from differences in bracketry to accommodate different seats and tanks, there really was little to

The 1955 Indian 500cc Tomahawk, a lightly restyled Royal Enfield 500 Twin. A HERL INC

In the background is the Indian Trailblazer (based on the Meteor/Super Meteor). At the front is the Chief, based on the Constellation, with 16in wheels. A HERL INC

The Italian-built 750 Indian with Interceptor power.

differentiate them from the equivalent Enfields. The high handlebars were predictable, but the new timing covers with Indian badging were a nice touch and the Chief did look the part. Brockhouse must have been pleased that it had resisted Clymer's charms.

Or perhaps not, because in 1960 Brockhouse sold the Indian name to AMC (Associated Motor Cycles), which owned Norton and Matchless, and decided to market the latter in the USA as Indians. But AMC had serious money problems and Clymer leapt at the chance finally to own the Indian name, buying it in 1963 from the beleaguered AMC.

Initially, Clymer had a slightly odd view of how he might use the name. In 1967, he sold *Cycle* to fund a factory in Germany that would put the Münch Mammoth – a crazy NSU car-engined motorcycle – into production. Part of the deal was that Münch would also build him a new motorcycle powered by the old Indian side-valve V-twin. Most of the first year's Mammoth production went to the USA badged as Clymer Münch, selling well despite costing over double what Honda was asking for its new 4-cylinder game changer. But dealers were not interested in the odd-looking side-valve Indian. Clymer needed a change of tack. His gaze settled on the Italjet Grifon and he flew to Bologna to meet its creator, the versatile Leopoldo Tartarini.

THE ITALIAN CONNECTION – CLYMER'S INDIANS WITH INTERCEPTOR POWER

Few men in motorcycling led as full a life as the genial Leopoldo Tartarini, universally known as Poldino and the founder of Italjet, the small but highly innovative Italian manufacturer established in 1960.

Tartarini's motorcycle career began at the age of twenty in 1952, when he won the sidecar class in the gruelling 18-hour single-stage Milano–Taranto open-roads marathon, beating the favoured Moto Guzzi and Gilera-powered competition with a twin-cylinder BSA 650 Golden Flash-engined outfit that he'd designed and built. The following year he won the 125cc class of the race on a Benelli Leoncino two-stroke that he had prepared himself and winning the Motogiro d'Italia outright that same year on the same bike. By the time a Ducati franchise was added to the family business Poldino was racing for the factory, before embarking upon

a year-long around the world trip aboard Ducati 175s in the company of Ducati's export sales manager, Giorgio Monetti.

Once back home in 1960, Tartarini decided to build his own motorcycles to sell in his Benelli and Ducati dealership. He founded Italemmezeta (ItalMZ), using East German motors. Rechristened Italjet Moto when he was commissioned by BSA-Triumph to develop a replacement for the BSA Bantam, the project never reached production, although it did introduce Tartarini to the British firm and eventually led to the Italjet Grifo 500 being shown at the 1965 Milan Show. This was a Triumph Tiger 100 engine fitted in a twin-loop Italjet frame, producing an Italian-built production version of the Triton. However, the 500 Grifo never reached production, partly because the name was already taken by rivals Guazzoni. Tartarini resolved that problem by adding an 'n', while also deciding that the relaunch would use the 650cc Bonneville motor.

The Grifon's combination of crisp Italian styling, chassis design flair and British engine performance brought Italjet to the attention of Floyd Clymer, who initially commissioned Tartarini to manufacture 100 Minarelli-engined 50cc minibikes for him to give as gifts to the US dealers he'd signed up to distribute his Indian V-twin. In keeping with the Indian theme, these were named the Papoose and proved so successful that Italjet ended up building more than 15,000 for the US market.

Reviewing the Triumph T120-powered Italjet Grifon, Clymer noted that it was actually slightly heavier that the lithe Bonneville but realized this would not be true if he used the Royal Enfield Interceptor's 736cc twin. Apart from the rather clunky Albion gearbox, there was nothing wrong with the Royal Enfield's comprehensively redesigned Series 2 power plant. It was just that the cycle parts and styling were rather old fashioned and heavy. The frames still used keystone joints and a single down tube, ideas that went back to flat tankers.

Instead, Tartarini went for a much lighter all-welded twin down-tube layout that allowed a short swinging arm with snail cam-chain adjustment. This was treated to Grimeca brakes, plus Borrani rims, Marzocchi forks and a style makeover that allowed the Indian to look half the weight of the Enfield, although the truth was 16lb (7.3kg): still a worthwhile saving over the donor bike's claimed wet weight of 410lb (186kg). Contemporary testers loved the new Indian and could reach almost 120mph (193km/h) with its 30mm Dell Orto carburettors. These were instead of Enfield's 30mm Amal concentrics. Other Italjet upgrades included 12V twin-coil ignition rather than a 6V magneto.

How many of these motorcycles were built or even planned is moot. Some say that 200 of the 750 engines were ordered from Enfield, others 600. In the end perhaps as few as thirty were assembled. Clymer died unexpectedly in January 1970 at the age of seventy-four and the new Indian range died with him. The unused Enfield engines were sold on to the Rickman Brothers for what they called the Rickman Enfield Interceptor and everyone else calls a Metisse. It is arguable that Royal Enfield could have soldiered on to get its 800 on sale if Clymer had not passed away, but with him went the Indian dream (for the time being at least), followed in 1971 by Enfield.

Floyd Clymer deserves credit for allowing Italjet to create these motorcycles. They were unequivocal improvements on the motorcycles they shared engines with and managed to look modern, stylish and yet traditional. They were intended to be high-quality, high-end products – the 750 and Velocette Thruxton-powered 500 both cost more than a Honda CB750 – and Italjet delivered on those promises. Their engines even seemed less prone to leaking oil than the English equivalents. It is a shame that Clymer could not have lived another few years to see them find a niche in Europe as well as America.

Happy Indian – and inadvertently Royal Enfield – owners. A HERL INC

Another Tartarini 750 Indian on the Bristol Classic Motor Cycle Show's Royal Enfield stand.

THE FINAL CHAPTER: THE RICKMAN INTERCEPTOR

After the death of Floyd Clymer in early 1970 the Rickman brothers Don and Derek acquired the remaining Enfield motors originally intended for Italjet's Indian 750s. The engines were held by importer-exporters Mitchells in Birmingham waiting to be shipped to Italy. Mitchells and the company receivers wanted to liquidate their new-found asset as soon as possible and approached famous frame-makers the Rickman brothers to see if a deal could be struck. Given that the Rickmans had just shown a new Interceptor-powered model it seemed likely it could be.

Don and Derek had started out with home-brewed TriBSAs – Triumph motors in BSA Gold Star frames – for the 1959 scrambles season. The bikes and the brothers proved seriously competitive from the off and a MkII version, with lightweight fibreglass bodywork designed by Doug Mitchenall of Avon Fairings, soon followed. The Rickmans' original plan was to sell their ideas and techniques to one of the big British factories, but when none showed any interest the Rickmans instead started building their own complete motorcycles using components from other motorcycle manufacturers. They fell upon using the name Métisse, amused that the French used the word to mean a mongrel, although it has other less savoury connotations. Proving they had a sense of humour, the Rickmans knew others would say that their bikes were mongrels, but their riposte would be that the Métisse proved there were good engines and good frames, but that the two were rarely put together.

Then, at London's Earls Court Motorcycle Show in 1962, the Rickmans showed off the next generation of the Métisse, with the Rickmans' own frame rather than the Gold Star item used for the original. Launching themselves into manufacturing chassis kits, the Rickmans took on a factory unit at Gore Road in New Milton, Hampshire, and set about satisfying a growing demand for their products. Before long, the Rickmans were offering Métisse chassis kits to suit a variety of British twins and singles; and, by 1965, Bultaco-powered Métisses, too. The diversification into a road bike wasn't far

The Rickman motorcycle with Royal Enfield Interceptor Mark II power. MOTACILLA

The nickel-plate frame was a Rickman trademark. BONHAMS

behind, the Rickmans working with London dealer and race team owner Tom Kirby to develop a road-racing chassis. Bill Ivy, who tested the new bike, was delighted with the handling of the new frame and the disc front brake the Rickmans had developed alongside AP Lockheed engineers.

So, building on their off-road success, Don and Derek now offered an off the shelf road racer, buying in G50 500cc singles from AMC to create the Matchless Rickman Métisse G50 short circuit and TT racer for 1964. The lightweight nickel-plated frame was claimed, in full racing specification with magnesium alloy yokes, to be 11.5lb (5.5kg) lighter and to carry the motor 1in (25mm) lower than the stock bike.

Other Rickman innovations included the use of large diameter telescopic forks, oil carried in the frame to help dissipate heat and save weight, and chain adjustment via eccentric discs rather than drawbolts so as to avoid misalignment. The first examples used AMC front forks and brakes, the latter fitted with a large cooling disc, although the Rickmans soon developed their own forks. The addition of Lockheed disc brakes was a first for both road racing and production motorcycles, the road bikes being the first to use disc brakes both front and

rear. The Métisse started to garner a number of road-racing victories, John Hartle's third spot in the 1967 world championship being the most notable.

The successful new frame was soon adapted to take other engines, including the Triumph twin, and it would serve as the basis of the road-going 'Street Métisse' café racer. An 8-valve cylinder head conversion with 700cc capacity based on the Triumph motor was developed, which increased power output to 60bhp or more. Launched at the 1966 Earls Court Motorcycle Show, where *Motorcycle News* offered the first model completed as a prize in their road safety competition, the Street Métisse was an instant hit. And, if it needed a publicity boost it soon had one, when Giacomo Agostini ordered one, collecting it at the TT in 1968. As the new decade of the 1970s dawned, the brothers were at it again, diversifying into the production of complete Rickman Zundapp and Rickman Montessa enduro and motocross machines.

By the time they were offered the Interceptor Series 2 motors the Rickman brothers' frames were – to the cognoscenti at least – world famous and they were ready to build their next production roadster, the Rickman Interceptor.

The elegant swan-neck handlebars offer adjustment and reasonable comfort. BONHAMS

They had already produced a number of prototypes in 1969, showing one at London's Racing and Sporting Show in January 1970, just as Floyd Clymer died. The Enfield-powered Métisse certainly looked the part and public reaction was positive enough to persuade the brothers to put a road-going version of the bike into production. Using the wet-sump Series 2 Interceptor engine negated the need for the Rickmans' trademark oil in frame layout, but the structure was still based on the tried and tested racing and Street Métisse. The basic design needed a little fine-tuning to accommodate the bulkier – compared to a Triumph 650 twin – Series 2 Interceptor engine, but not much. Retaining the geometry of the road racers, this new frame with wider spaced bottom rails allowed the crankcases of the Interceptor engine to fit between them and so place the engine lower in the frame to bring down the centre of gravity. Fabricated using hand-brazed, chrome-molybdenum Reynolds 531 tubing and finished in the traditional Rickman polished nickel plate, the frame of the Rickman Interceptor was a work of art. But

The Métisse moniker was a tongue in cheek choice by the Rickman brothers – French for mongrel. BONHAMS

it was also supremely functional and massively strong, the Rickmans' race-proven geometry delivering on-rails security when cornering and high-speed stability. Despite such a sturdy frame, the Rickmans' Interceptor-powered special weighed 60lb (28kg) less than a standard Series 2, with attention to detail exemplified by the precise drive-chain adjustment effected by eccentric discs at the swinging-arm spindle.

The rest of the bike was similarly well specified, with Rickman forks taking care of business up front – although Italian Ceriani units were fitted to some bikes – while the Lockheed disc brakes front and rear were a marked improvement over the Norton drums used on the standard Series 2 Interceptor. Anodized Rickman hubs and Italian Borrani alloy rims completed the specification of the rolling chassis. There were unusual, inverted swan-neck clip-on handlebars, similar to those on the Moto Guzzi V7 Sport. These, combined with the rider's footrests being attached directly to the exhaust pipes, provided a sporty, rather than radical, riding position. The Rickman Interceptor was unmistakable on the road, especially with the later striking orange colour scheme, although early examples were blue, and red was also an option for the high-quality fibreglass bodywork.

There were seven prototypes made (frame numbers R650, 651, 652, 797, 810, 811 and 979), so when Indian's receivers got in touch it was serendipitous indeed. The Rickmans were in need of Interceptor motors and suddenly 200 or so were made available at the drop of a hat. Between April 1970 and January 1972, some 130 to 138 Rickman Enfields were produced, making them rare and highly sought-after today. There were, however, only 130 production Rickmans originally made. Production went from April 1970 until January 1972. Frame numbers commenced at R1001 and ran through to R1130.

A few were sold in the USA and Canada, where prospective purchasers were tempted by the offer of a spare engine for just $550 ($600 in Canada) and all seem to have had the Ceriani forks. In the UK, south-west London dealers Elite Motors signed up to handle retail sales, rather than buyers ordering directly from the Rickman factory. The first few bikes had actually trickled out on to the market in 1970, but Elite became the sole distributor in early 1971. By then, Honda's game-changing CB750 – with its 4-cylinder ohc engine, electric start and slick five-speed gearbox – had hit the streets and motorcycling was changing. The Honda cost £719 in 1971 and the Rickman Interceptor was initially priced at £750, meaning that sales of the Rickman Enfield were sluggish to say the least. By 1974, when the last of the production run was finally sold, the price had come down to £550, while the CB750 had gone up to £979 and Kawasaki's new Z1 was £1,177. Suddenly the Rickman Interceptor seemed a bargain, but, with the supply of engines having dried up, there would be no more.

Around fifty of the bikes are thought still to exist, making them a desirable if pretty rare bird. The beefy Royal Enfield motor offered bags of torque aided by a claimed weight of just 365lb (165kg). Compared to the Royal Enfield version's 426lb (193kg), this makes the Métisse arguably the best of the British big twins. Even the brakes were good. Its only real failings were the antiquated clutch and gearbox and the fact that riders were becoming used to an electric starter. It also, initially at least, cost more than the Honda CB750. However, fifty years on from its launch, that doesn't really matter anymore. If you like big, lusty Brit twins, they don't get much better than the Rickman Interceptor, or its Italian cousin the Indian 750 – although they will still cost you more than a CB750.

9

POST-WAR COMPETITION SUCCESS

Richard Stevens racing the factory Interceptor Series 2. RICHARD STEVENS' COLLECTION

As the class horsepower leader, the Constellation should have been a good choice for production racing, but the promise was never fully realized. Constellations were usually the fastest bikes in the field, but frequently retired with mechanical issues. The closest Royal Enfield came to a significant victory was in 1958, when Enfield dealer Syd Lawton entered a Constellation in the 500-mile (805km) endurance race at Thruxton with riders Bob McIntyre and Derek Powell. Though they recorded faster times on the track than the eventual winners (Mike Hailwood and Dan Shorey on a Triumph 650), McIntyre and Powell lost time in the pits, handing the race to their rivals.

As the adage goes, to finish first, first you have to finish, and too often the big Enfield twins didn't. Factory tester Richard Stevens raced the Interceptor, but was brutally honest about its chances. 'I think the Bonneville was the better bike,' he admits. 'It was the machine to have in production racing at the time. It was a better package, with good handling.' Further proof that races aren't run on dynamometers came later when Richard proved quicker on a 30bhp Suzuki Super Six than he had on an Interceptor with almost twice the power.

Even with the singles, Royal Enfield struggled with road racing. It has never won a TT and the few podium places were won pre-war. In the modern era Royal Enfield classic racers have again struggled, even in the hands of legends such as the father and son team of Steve and Olie Linsdell. Perhaps that's because the competition bikes were aimed at off-road heroism, as that's where the Smith family's passion really lay.

OFF-ROAD

The Bullet could be had in road, trials, or scrambles versions, with equipment and gearing to suit the application, but the new prototype Bullet first broke ground as a 346cc trials bike, ridden by a works trio at the Colmore Cup Trial. While unsuccessful on its initial appearance, the newest Royal Enfield soon showed its form with Bullet-mounted riders winning gold medals later in 1948 in the ISDT, an important part of the winning British Trophy team. The Bullet's ISDT debut in San Remo, in the Ligure Italian Alps, saw two of these new models, ridden by Vic Brittain and Charlie Rogers, selected by the ACU to represent Great Britain in the Trophy award team. Chosen for the Vase award team was Jack Stocker, on the 500 Model J, the trio

of Royal Enfield pilots completing the course without losing any points. Making the time checks was especially difficult, conditions that year being so fast and hectic that the trial was nicknamed the Italian Grand Prix, and any machine with the stamina to survive such prolonged high-speed hammering on rough tracks was worthy of high praise. Great Britain won the coveted Trophy, providing a significant boost to British prestige and sales opportunities. That the Bullet went so well off-road surprised many, because not everyone agreed that a rear swinging arm was a good idea. Until the Bullet, trials bikes had rigid rear frames, favoured for their light weight and predictable handling.

Both Brittain and Rogers had represented their country in pre-war ISDT, although Brittain had already decided that 1948 would be his final year of competing. The British win meant that Rogers elected to carry on for one more year and 1949 again found him a member of the victorious British Trophy team, on his 350 Bullet. Stocker was again chosen for the Vase team and these two – in company with Stan Holmes – won a Manufacturer's Team award for Royal Enfield.

Following British success in San Remo, the 1949 ISDT was staged in Wales, as it would be again in 1950 – and on both occasions five Royal Enfields came through with clean sheets (that is, no mistakes such as putting a foot down). This was a remarkable achievement in 1950, when appalling weather conditions meant that just thirty-eight gold medals were shared

The ex-Billy Mills 500 Bullet. He was a member of the Rhayader Motorcycle & Light Car Club together with his great friend Arthur Bates, another ISDT competitor, and they and ISDT Gold Medal winner John Lewis won several Special Gold Medals in the Welsh Three Days Trial. BONHAMS

In the 1952 ISDT, held at Bad Aussee in Austria, this 500 Twin was ridden by Johnny Brittain as part of the British Vase B team. Unfortunately, he was sidelined on the fifth day with engine failure. BONHAMS

among 213 starters. Now it was Stocker's turn to graduate to the Trophy team and British mastery of the sport was emphasized by a sweeping victory. Eighteen year-old Johnny Brittain – son of Vic – entered the team that year with his 350 Bullet, gaining a gold medal along with Stocker and Holmes. Easily the quickest 350s in the British team, these Bullets covered themselves in glory for 1948, 1949 and 1950.

TAKING THE 500 TWIN OFF-ROAD

Launched in 1948, Royal Enfield's twin was conventional enough, although as already noted the separate barrels and cylinder heads, and the oil tank within the crankcase – a feature inherited from the singles – was unusual. The new engine was installed in what was basically the Bullet frame, an advanced design featuring swinging-arm rear suspension. Royal Enfield's success in post-war trials owed much to this innovation, but also to the talents of works rider Johnny Brittain and the likes of Jack Stocker, Stan Holmes, Don Evans and Johnny's younger brother Pat.

For 1951, Royal Enfield, hungry for publicity, entered three 500 Twins, again ridden by Stocker, Holme and Brittain. The ISDT was held that year at Varese, Northern Italy, and some particularly vile road surfaces were encountered. The Great Britain team comprised Stocker on a 500 Twin, with Hugh Viney (AJS), Jim Alves (Triumph), Bob Ray (Ariel) and Fred Rist (BSA). The British team completed the trial without losing any marks, winning the International Trophy for Great Britain. The fourth 500 Twin was ridden by the Swedish Silver Vase team's Börje Nyström, who also won a gold medal. Capitalizing on this success, Stocker and his two team-mates were featured in Royal Enfield's post-ISDT advertising, sitting proudly on their mounts. One was also displayed on Royal Enfield's stand at the 1951 Motorcycle Show.

The British Trophy victory in 1951 meant that Great Britain was again entitled to organize 1952's ISDT, although the ACU declined the invitation, the event instead being held at Bad Aussee in Austria. Johnny Brittain, on a 500 Twin, was part of the British Vase B team, but he was sidelined on the fifth day with engine failure. Very extreme changes of temperature and almost unceasing rain resulted in wholesale loss of marks, yet, although Great Britain failed to bring

Twice World Champion for Moto Guzzi in the 350cc class (1955 and 1956), Bill Lomas built this Royal Enfield racer in the late 1940s. The machine consists of a pre-war frame, converted to swinging-arm rear suspension in 1948.
BONHAMS

Billy Mills was a successful businessman in Llandrindod Wells – he owned a local mineral water company, Tiara Soft Drinks – but spent much of his free time competing on this 500 Bullet. BONHAMS

Bill Lomas built his Royal Enfield racer with a 250cc ohv engine that he developed while working for Royal Enfield. Recognizing the pushrod engine's limitations, in 1949 Bill had designed and built a twin-cam cylinder head for the Enfield, inspired by the 250 Benelli. Having spent his National Service in the REME, Bill then landed a job in Royal Enfield's competitions department. BONHAMS

home the Trophy, a Royal Enfield was one of just three British machines in the class to finish a disastrous week unpenalized. This was Stocker aboard the new Meteor 700, yet another successful debut for a Royal Enfield in an ISDT.

Only twice, post-war, have two machines from the same factory been chosen to represent Great Britain in the Trophy team. In 1948, it had been Vic Brittain and Charlie Rogers on their 350 Bullets, and for 1953 it was Jack Stocker and Johnny Brittain – now a hardened veteran of twenty-one – who were entrusted to regain the ISDT Trophy. In addition to the two Trophy teamsters, Don Evans was chosen to represent Great Britain in the Vase team. All three riders were mounted on 500 Twins for the event in Czechoslovakia.

All six Enfields entered in the ISDT completed the 1,500-mile (2,415km) course despite the highest average speed ever required in the event – all without mechanical trouble, although Swedish team member Ake Elgebrandt and his 500 Bullet were caught up in a group of struggling competitors on a particularly difficult hill climb. The delay cost him marks for a late arrival at the next checkpoint and the chance of a gold medal.

Aside from this, the 1953 ISDT was a triumph for Royal Enfield riders and for Great Britain. Victorious in sixteen of the twenty-eight ISDTs to date, the British Trophy team finished an action-packed week unscathed. As a member of the winning team, Stocker collected his sixth successive gold medal and, with Brittain and Evans, again won a Manufacturer's Team Prize: the third for Royal Enfield over a five-year period. The total haul included five gold medals and one silver medal, and two Royal Enfields had completed ISDTs without the loss of a single mark. Between them, Royal Enfields, ranging from Frank Carey's eleven year-old 350cc sidecar outfit to Jack Stocker's box-fresh Meteor 700, had covered close on 70,000 racing miles (112,654km).

A STAR IS BORN

When Johnny Brittain joined Royal Enfield in 1950, the company finally had a superstar who could sprinkle the motorcycles in showrooms with stardust. He was born John Victor Brittain to 1920s and 1930s hero Vic Brittain, himself a multifaceted rider who had successfully competed in everything from ISDTs to TT races, scrambles and fairground daredevil stunts, and who had been persuaded to come out of retirement and join Enfield for one year in order to ride a Bullet in the 1948 ISDT.

Johnny and his younger brother Pat grew up in Walsall, where their father ran a garage and motor engineering business and where Johnny would begin his working life on leaving school. Despite his father's successes, there was no pressure to take up motorcycling and in the immediate post-war period fuel was in any case in such short supply that the local motorcycle club added bicycle trials to their events roster. Brittain's success with pedal power led to local motorcycle manufacturer DMW (Dawson Motor Works) offering him a ride in the national Clayton Trial.

From this tentative beginning, an entry was gained with James motorcycles for the 125cc class of the 1949 ISDT, which would be held in Wales, thanks to the British Team having won the 1948 San Remo event, with Johnny's father Vic part of the winning Trophy Team. Johnny repaid their confidence by winning a gold, his first of thirteen such medals in ISDTs, beating the three James works riders in the process. At eighteen, Johnny moved into the big time with Royal Enfield, by now his contemporaries calling him JV, although to the readers of the motorcycling press he would become simply Johnny. A lanky, quietly spoken and studious young man, he was the product of the age and very different to the assured media savvy individuals that we are used to today. But put him on a motorcycle and point him at a dirt track and there was a Jekyll and Hyde transformation. He quickly went from being the youngster to watch to being the man to beat, with first-class awards in one-day trials and a gold

medal in the 1950 ISDT. *The Motorcycle* and *Motorcycling* both loved him and would gushingly report his every word:

> *In the early days my competitors openly ridiculed me, deriding the spring-frame Bullet. They were still on rigid-framed bikes and would say things like: 'I pity you having to ride that Enfield with that bouncy rear suspension.' They were soon laughing on the other side of their faces when I began winning, and it took several years for all the other manufacturers to catch up and adopt the Bullet's swinging-arm suspension, which gave me a real edge.*

Clearly Johnny was modest too.

On his famous 350cc trials Bullet, registration number HNP 331, Johnny won the prestigious Scottish Six Days' Trial in 1952 and 1957, a gruelling 900-mile (1,450km) contest. He also won the British Experts Trial in 1952 and 1953, becoming its youngest ever winner, and the arduous Scott Trial in 1955 and 1956. There were over fifty major championship wins and a sackful of open trial first places. Beginning with his first ISDT campaign on a Royal Enfield in the 1950 competition, Johnny accumulated thirteen gold medals over fifteen years, although some of those rides were on a 500 Twin and a 500 Bullet rather than HNP 331.

Johnny Brittain's works trials Bullets of 1956 and 1957 were all-conquering. In 1956, he triumphed in the ACU Star championship and his tally of wins included the Welsh Trophy, the Scott, Mitchell and Streatham trials, the Alan Hurst, Shropshire and Patland Cups, as well as second places in the Scottish Six Days' Trial and two other major events. The following year, he clocked up wins in the Scottish Six Days' Vic Brittain event – named in honour of his father – alongside Cleveland, Travers, Red Rose and Cotswold Trials, amongst others.

To mark this remarkable run of achievements, Enfield released the 350 Trials Works Replica closely based on his 1958 machine. Using the same lightweight, all-welded frame made of aircraft-quality chrome-molybdenum, it sported a slimmed-down 2½gal (11ltr) petrol tank, 21in front wheel, knobbly tyres, alloy mudguards, a sump guard, high-level exhaust, Lucas Wader magneto and a slimline gearbox with low gearing. The engine was given the works treatment with the bottom end built around the meatier 500cc Bullet flywheels, with fabulous low rpm control, and an aluminium alloy barrel.

Although he was the star, Johnny was not Royal Enfield's only trials rider. There was always a works team at major events, which, over the years, included Johnny's younger brother, Pat, as well as luminaries such as Tom Ellis, 'Jolly Jack' Stocker, Don Evans, Peter Fletcher, Peter Gaunt and Peter Stirland. Even Bill Lomas, long before he became a double Grand Prix world champion, won a first-class award on a Royal Enfield trials Bullet.

The ex-works, Jack Stocker, 1951 ISDT gold medal-winning 1951 Royal Enfield 495cc Twin. BONHAMS

Bill Lomas won the Cadwell Park 250cc Championship with this machine in 1948, 1949 and 1950, and his excellent results at the Lincolnshire track and other British circuits led to offers of rides in Grands Prix and at the Isle of Man TT. BONHAMS

By the end of the 1950s, however, the days of the heavyweight trials motorcycle were numbered. Responding to the trend for ever lighter bikes, with revvier engines that could snap the front wheel up and over obstacles and make best use of the constantly improving tyre compounds and tread patterns, Royal Enfield refocused its trials ambitions around the new, unit-construction 250cc Crusader.

Over the following decades many owners have created their own Bullet trials bikes, using both British and Indian roadster singles as their starting point. Although the majority have standard gearing and see only occasional light green-laning use, a significant number have been built to fully competitive specification and are regular entrants in classic trials events, including the celebrated Scottish Pre-65 Trial, a revered annual competition held in the highlands of Scotland ahead of the Scottish Six Days' Trial.

THE OFF-ROAD CRUSADER

Royal Enfield's Bullet had proved an outstanding trials motorcycle, but, by the early 1960s, the days of such heavyweights were numbered. Lightweights were now seen as the way forward, so the Redditch factory turned to the only suitable machine in its range: the 250 Crusader. A works Crusader prototype first competed in the late 1950s with mixed results and it was not until 1960 that Irishman Benny Crawford brought the marque its first major success, winning the Irish national championship, a feat he repeated the following year. The Crawford-developed production version debuted at the Motorcycle Show in the autumn of 1961, the works riders for the 1962 season being Enfield stalwarts Johnny Brittain and Peter Fletcher.

In his book *Classic British Trials Bikes*, renowned sports photographer and authority on off-road competition motorcycles Don Morley wrote that: 'any of the Crusader 250 machines can be converted to trials specification quite easily'; indeed, he had done so himself using a roadster as the basis. Don's regular appearance in classic off-road events meant choosing a Crusader because 'the Royal Enfields in 250cc and 350cc form handled better than any other bike of the era'.

Perhaps the off-road Crusader's brightest moment in the sun was, like many other motorcycles, as a TV star on Saturday afternoon sports programmes. These would switch with unbelievable eclecticism from sports such as darts, horse racing, wrestling to, occasionally – to the delight of motorcycle fans – motorcycle competition. The first televised scramble took place at Beenham, near Reading, in December 1954 and, as one might expect with off-road racing at that time of year, the muddy conditions made life extremely difficult and the meeting occurred over a shorter course than normally used by the South Reading club.

The BBC had previously successfully televised live speedway and road racing, but the difficulty of covering an off-road event like scrambling meant that this had never previously been tried. The world's first newspaper TV critic, Leonard Marsland Gander of the *Daily Telegraph*, wrote: 'Obviously the sport has exciting possibilities but viewers will need to know more about it before they really take it to their hearts.'

Clearly the viewers enjoyed it, because, after both the BBC and ITV had flirted with the coverage of scrambles for some years, the BBC Grandstand Trophy, with commentator Murray Walker, became compulsive Saturday viewing, loved by millions when the series aired from 1963 until 1970.

Unsurprisingly then, this is where Royal Enfield targeted Peter Fletcher's efforts, especially as Johnny Britain approached retirement and increasing financial difficulties

A 1960 Crusader converted to compete in trials.
BONHAMS

made sending a works teams overseas to compete in ISDT an unjustifiable expense. But the Crusader, even heavily modified most notably with leading link forks and Armstrong suspension, was no match for the new breed of two-strokes. Royal Enfield had one last fling with a Villiers Starmaker-powered motocrosser offered between 1963 and 1965. The designer of the 247cc two-stroke single, Bernard Hooper, was interviewed in 1983 and reflected that:

As a scrambles engine the Starmaker was way ahead of its time. This was to be the first of a new generation of Villiers two-strokes, breaking away from the old 34A type sloggers, and approaching the motocross engines of today. But the difficulty was that we were building it for weekend riders, and they just weren't ready for it; this unit required new riding skills, new expertise and a lack of nerve.

Hooper expanded on this:

I can remember one key winter scrambles, at Rollswood Farm, when to everybody's surprise Chris Horsfield, on a Starmaker-powered James, beat the great BSA hero, Jeff Smith. He achieved this, in the slippery conditions, by feeling his way out of the bends and controlling the bike on the throttle. The average British motocross competitor just wasn't used to this technique, but today it's accepted practice.

A peaky two-stroke, giving up low-end torque in exchange for top-end power, might have been a new idea off-road, but was long accepted in road racing. So it came as no surprise when various British factories, including Cotton, Dot and Greeves, took the Starmaker to the short circuits of the UK. Racers used to highly strung two-strokes had no problem with what the engine's designer called 'a lack of nerve'.

The first of these road-racing machines was the Cotton Telstar, then its sister, the Cotton Conquest, followed, both ridden by Derek Minter. His achievements were continued by his co-rider Peter Inchley, who would later create his own work of art, 'The Villiers Special'. However, the Starmaker then also started to succeed in its intended sport, motocross. But Royal Enfield's Starmaker motocrosser was quietly dropped and instead efforts were focused on the GP5 road racer.

THE GP5

Having noted the success of the Greeves Silverstone, Royal Enfield decided that it deserved a share of the emerging clubman's racer market and began work on a 250 race bike of its own. Geoff Duke was hired as project consultant in 1964 and Reynolds' Ken Sprayson came up with a fine duplex loop frame, but the prototype was let down by the poor performance of its underdeveloped Villiers Starmaker engine. Seeking a solution, Enfield turned to two-stroke guru Hermann Meier, who had prepared the Ariel Arrow ridden by Mike O'Rourke to a sensational seventh place in the 1960 Lightweight TT.

But rather than being given the free hand he expected, Meier was told to keep costs down and use products from within the E. & H.P. Smith Group, Enfield's increasingly disinterested owners. Meier particularly hated the Alpha crankcase assembly and was also lumbered with an Albion gearbox and a clutch based on that of Enfield's roadster twins. Using a Meier-designed cylinder with four, rather than the conventional two, transfer ports, the GP5 engine produced respectable power – a claimed 34bhp with the works bikes reaching 36bhp, more than the contemporary Silverstone – yet results on the race track were disappointing, to say the least. Only on one occasion did the bike show its true potential, when Percy Tait finished third behind the works Yamahas of Phil Read and Mike Duff in the 1965 Hutchinson 100 at Silverstone.

Royal Enfield rapidly progressed to making the GP5 one of the best-handling and most powerful British 250s ever built. The story started on a high note, with *Motor Cycling* announcing in 1964 'Hartle to Ride 250 Royal Enfield Works Racer' and going on to write:

> *Royal Enfield's road racing comeback – presaged last October by their joint managing director Leo Davenport – took a dramatic step forward last week when 1960 Junior TT winner John Hartle agreed to test their prototype 250 at Oulton Park early next month.*
>
> *'Moon Eyes' John Cooper was one of the top riders to campaign the Royal Enfield racer. Others included Percy Tait and Griff Jenkins.*
>
> *John said: 'The prototype sounds very good. It has a special frame and forks built for Royal Enfield by Reynolds, and the engine will be one of the latest single-carburettor Starmaker units.'*
>
> *John is due to visit the Redditch factory to see the machine being prepared and to discuss racing matters with Leo Davenport, winner of the 1932 Lightweight TT. Royal Enfield is being advised on their re-entry into racing by another very famous TT winner – six-time World Champion Geoff Duke.*

Another report seemed optimistic: 'Coming along nicely is the prototype Royal Enfield racer which John Hartle may ride in the Hutchinson 100 meeting at Silverstone on April 4.' But it added ominously that: 'The final decision cannot yet be made because John has other commitments.' It was a *Motor Cycle News* headline: 'Hartle's First – and Last – Ride on the Enfield Racer?' that outlined those commitments. The story went:

> *Hartle's oil company commitments are with a different concern to those of Royal Enfield's, and this is almost certain to prevent him from racing this works prototype production racer. He has been entered on the 250 Enfield by Geoff Duke for the Hutchinson 100 meeting at Silverstone on Saturday 4 April, but it seems now that there will be a change of rider.*

The writing was on the wall for the GP5 project; Royal Enfield was in financial difficulty and the racing department

The GP5 Villiers 250-based road racer. BONHAMS

was closed to save money. The GP5 remains yet another 'what might have been' in the history of the British racing two-stroke. Engine numbers of known survivors suggest that around thirty were made.

Mick Walker believed there was potential worth pursuing, but realistically Enfield was right to abandon the project. In 1958, Yamaha produced the YD1, the company's first 250cc motorcycle and a machine that would come to be recognized as the father of all future Yamaha two-strokes. When Yamaha introduced the TZ's predecessors, the 1963 TD1 and especially its successor the 1965 TR2B, the future of road racing changed forever. These machines were more than capable of outperforming any British single of whatever capacity in all respects except perhaps absolute top speed on Isle of Man gearing. In 1965, the Suzuki (Super Six in the UK) T20 was the first six-speed motorcycle to go into production, and to Richard Stevens, used to racing an Interceptor with its clumsy Albion gearbox, it was a revelation.

Finally, in 1967 the much less troublesome Yamaha TD1-C appeared, filling the racetrack grids of the world. Even if Royal Enfield had had more money and luck with the GP5 and could have found a replacement for the Albion gearbox, it is hard to see why anyone would have chosen it over the Yamaha, especially once Colin Seeley started building frames for the Japanese bike.

A METAPHOR FOR THE END OF ROYAL ENFIELD

The GP5 really was a metaphor for the British motorcycle industry: too little, too late and failing to appreciate how quickly the Japanese were upping their game. The make do and mend philosophy of the British factories worked when the competition was building essentially the same products from the same components in factories that had all been starved of investment for decades. Competing with clean-sheet designs – often cherry picking the best ideas wherever they might be found – built on modern production lines in purpose-built factories was always going to end badly. The truth is that, as the then head of Honda UK, Gerald Davison, once said to me, the British were too small to compete with the Japanese by the mid-1950s. And others – notably Ducati – who did try to offer a motorcycle in every sector, even in their protected home market, could not compete with the Japanese and eventually thrived only by building a premium product. Could the British have done the same?

There are plenty of armchair management consultants who opine that the death of the British motorcycle industry was inevitable from the point at which it started to ignore the commuters and middleweight riders who represented the future buyers of heavyweight motorcycles. Indeed, Sir Bernard Docker had been lobbying, notably via the *Financial Times*, for shareholders and government tax collectors to reign in their expectations if BSA was to have enough cash to invest in new models and factories from the mid-1950s onward. He was probably right, but, as to taking on the Japanese 250–350 class, he was already too late. The history of the British motorcycle factories and, more intriguingly, erstwhile survivors Harley-Davidson, is where fans of Western lightweights that might avoid sector retreat from the Japanese – and later others from Asia – are proved wrong.

Harley-Davidson spent the late 1960s and much of the 1970s trying to stick to the accepted wisdom of fighting the Japanese motorcycle industry at all levels. Then owned by the AMF conglomerate, Harley bought up Aermacchi, developed a range of affordable two-stroke motorcycles from 125 to 350cc, and promoted them by winning 250 and 350 road-racing world championships. In the USA, the company developed road racers based upon its iconic V-twins, notably Lucifer's Hammer, and campaigned endlessly to make sure that its motorcycles had every chance to sell well and win races. But, despite successful government and AMA (American Motorcycle Association) lobbying (unlike the far less-dynamic British motorcycle industry), Harley continued to lose money by building motorcycles that were overpriced for what they offered and underprepared for what buyers in the 1970s expected of a brand-new machine.

In despair, AMF sold the company in 1981 to a team led by Vaughn Beals and Willie G. Davidson for $80 million. Beals was from a commercial diesel engine and logging machinery background, although Davidson was Harley-Davidson royalty. The team threw away the received wisdom, which they realized was based upon building motorcycles in the sort of numbers they would never be able to achieve. Instead, they pursued what they did well, making sure that money was never wasted, including copying Japanese production techniques such as the 'just in time' delivery model. More cash was spent ensuring that the bikes were properly screwed together, making for happy customers and minimal warranty claims.

I once asked Gerald Davison, having seen Honda become a global colossus, if he'd thought the British motorcycle industry could have been saved. He didn't hesitate:

Oh yes, of course. Go niche, but do it quickly. By the time Honda had arrived in the UK they were already the biggest factory in the world. The British were never going to beat them. But there would still be a market for sectors that the Japanese would never find profitable.

Ironically, unlike the other British factories – notably BSA – Royal Enfield did not go bust trying to compete; it just stopped digging the hole the industry was in. Having given up on Royal Enfield, E. & H.P. Smith focused on Amalgamated Industrials, purchased just after their acquisition of the Redditch works, eventually taking the name for themselves: the business still exists. Down in Bradford-on-Avon, it was the same story for Enfield Precision Engineering. There was too much lucrative work coming in from the Ministry of Defence to bother with motorcycles that nobody would buy at the sort of price Enfield needed them to pay. Ironically, Royal Enfield was almost uniquely placed to offer a hand-built motorcycle and price it to compete with, say, a Ducati 900SS or Laverda Jota, but in truth why bother? To compete with the Japanese would have meant multimillion-pound investments in new factories. The alternative, which would gradually occur to business, was off-shoring, moving factories to countries where wages are far lower than in the West. The irony is that Royal Enfield had already unwittingly done that and so the name survives.

Geoff Duke on the GP5 in front of the factory, roof tiles picked out to announce Royal Enfield's home. The offices are to the right. ROYAL ENFIELD

The GP5's top end was bespoke, but the bottom end was Villiers and the gearbox Albion. BONHAMS

10

REMEMBERING THE BRITISH FACTORIES

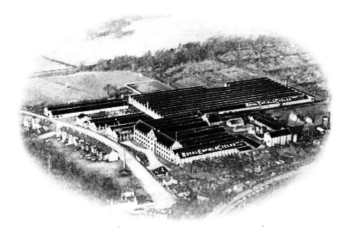

THE ENFIELD CYCLE C.º L.ᵀᴰ

HEAD OFFICE & WORKS

REDDITCH

Telephone : Redditch 122 (5 lines)   Telegrams : "Cycles, Redditch"

A 1920s catalogue cover with an aerial view of the Redditch works.

There is a great irony about Anne Bradford's wonderful book *Royal Enfield: The Story of the Company and the People Who Made it Great: 1851–1969*, which recounts interviews

with many of the Redditch factory's workers during the early 1990s. The book was written because Anne lives in what looks like the original Givry needle works, which later became the first Royal Enfield factory in Hunt End. A local historian, Anne only discovered the industrial heritage literally on her doorstep because a succession of Royal Enfield fans knocked on her door asking about her house and the industrial estate opposite. In fact, the needle works burned down and was replaced with houses that mimicked the look of the Givry factory.

On the other side of what is now called Enfield Road – it seems sad that changing the name of Hunt End to this was thought to be a tribute – was the new Hunt End works, which Enfield quickly outgrew. The Hunt End works were sold in 1919 to the UK subsidiary of the Swedish battery company A.B. Jungner under the name Batteries Ltd using the brand name NIFE. The buildings survived until the late 1960s, by then used by Dunlop to store tyres.

In another uncanny coincidence, when Royal Enfield closed in Redditch, Les 'Kipper' Gibbs, who had been with Royal Enfield since 1928, was lucky enough to find a job at Dunlop. One Saturday afternoon, Gibbs was the last one to depart the factory, leaving the caretaker behind him. The caretaker had a fondness for hot meals and used a stove inside an old tyre to heat his dinner. He fell asleep, woke with a start and fled the fire he'd started, raising the alarm. But the local water supply was at too low a pressure for the fire brigade, who had to bring water in bowsers. Tyre fires are notoriously hard to put out and at the fire's height the flames could be seen 3 miles (5km) away. But, at least, as Gibbs left on that fateful day it meant that a Royal Enfield man was the last to work at the premises, as well as the first.

By the time the fire brigade had done their work, the Hunt End works had been reduced to rubble. The only thing left standing was the bottom of the exterior wall, which has been preserved in memory of what was once standing there. Anne Bradford in another book, *Old Redditch Voices*, claims that people from all over the world come to take pictures of this wall. The rest of the site is now an industrial estate.

So really the story of Royal Enfield's motorcycle works starts with Factory Number 1, the main Royal Enfield works built on Hewell Road in 1907. This includes the iconic building with 'Royal Enfield' picked out in white-painted tiles on the roof. This was used as a backdrop for endless publicity shots, notably the photograph of Geoff Duke, immaculate as ever in a suit, astride the GP5 250 racer prototype. Along from this is a stretch of windows for the office staff to look out from, about 150 people including founding partner and joint managing director, Bob Walker Smith (but referred to as R.W. Smith by staff) and, from the end of the war his son, the Major, who had been joint managing director with his father since 1914. Here were the people who dealt with accounts, buying raw materials and paying wages.

But the concept of wages is rather different to today, with our many laws around employment contracts, redundancy and minimum wages taken for granted. Most people started work at age thirteen or fourteen, and if there was no work people were sent home unpaid: three-day weeks were commonplace over the autumn and winter. Many were paid piecework, a carry-over from cottage industry where workers were only paid for the number of pieces – wheels, sidecars, complete motorcycles – they made. In role reversal, there are stories of Royal Enfield workers clocking off when the factory closed at 5pm (work having started at 8am), surreptitiously taking small items home to work on overnight, thus boosting their pay.

But that's not to say businesses were ruthless exploiters of their employees. The Smith family were great supporters of the (now Royal) British Legion, established in 1921 to care for those who had suffered as a result of service during World War 1. Almost 200 Royal Enfield employees were members, raising money to alleviate post-war poverty and support those in greatest need.

An expansion of the Hewell Road plant took place towards the end of 1926. This took the plant to 9.7 hectares (24 acres), including sports facilities that extended to a cricket pitch, grass and hard tennis courts, and even waters reserved for fishing. And all of this was not just for motorcycle production: Enfield was still making components for others and still building several hundred complete bicycles every week, both being important to the company's profitability. The factory would still look Victorian to modern eyes, with women having to wear hats or scarves to prevent leather drive belts catching their long hair. The lack of a recognizable production line seems odd given that Bob Walker Smith was supposedly good friends with Henry Ford, but he was also very hands on. A problem in production would see him summoned and asked for ideas. Even when he notionally retired, Smith simply took a smaller office at the front of the building while his son moved into the managing director's office.

When Frank Walker Smith returned from the war, having served in the Royal Artillery and Flying Corps and being promoted to Major, he effectively took over as the man in charge. He was barely thirty years of age, but was much respected and known simply as the Major. He remained active in the Territorial Army and would command the local Home Guard in World War II. He rose to become president of the Birmingham Chamber of Commerce, a member of the council of the British Cycle and Motor Cycle Association, often handing out badges emblazoned with 'Buy British and support British Trade'. He was, as they would say back then, 'A Doer'. The CBE arrived in 1949.

By 1930, the Hewell Road site covered 7.3 hectares (18 acres), over 3 hectares (8 acres) of them glazed. There were now proper toilet and washing facilities, rather than a bucket proffered at the end of each shift. Smoking was banned and repeat offenders were fired: there was simply too great a risk of the factory burning down. A new building was also devoted to sidecars that accompanied most of the V-twins and plenty of the 350s. These were built of American white-wood and ply under the supervision of foreman Jack George. Revolutionarily, they attached to Enfield's motorcycles with just two bolts, one fore and aft, allowing the claim that they could be removed within a minute.

It was not just engines that Royal Enfield was taking in house, with a team of women spoking wheels. Other manufacturers would also use Royal Enfield's wheel building team, more than one of them ironically complaining that they hated working on Brough Superior's rims and spokes as being of 'the cheapest quality' and so difficult to assemble. This was not just a nuisance, since the wheel builders, like most in the factory, were paid on piecework rather than receiving a regular wage. These lost voices also give rise to questions as well as answers: in Anne Bradford's book one pieceworker complains about assembling the last complete motorcycles with Motosacoche engines in 'about 1925 or 1926'. This would be at least a decade after Royal Enfield is recorded as having dropped the Swiss motors and indeed after Motosacoche stopped selling engines branded as such: by 1925 the name was reserved for its own complete motorcycles and it was selling power units under the MAG brand. But, as we have seen, Royal Enfield did supply components to Motosacoche during World War I and so a quid pro quo may have been possible. It is also a warning that there is much in history that is uncertain and the claimant's assertion that the motor was a 424cc V-twin suggests it was actually one of Royal Enfield's own early motors. Could the resulting motorcycle have been branded Motosacoche? It's an intriguing idea.

In November 1926, disaster came close to striking. In the early hours of the 26th, a fire broke out in a sawmill and timber yard next to the works. The amateur but brave Enfield fire brigade, of which the Major was so proud, was able to keep the fire under control until the Redditch town

brigade arrived and the works survived unscathed. But again it emphasizes that Royal Enfield was a big family, often made up from people with big families – a dozen siblings wasn't unusual, living in cramped self-sufficiency. Some of the people who left when the Redditch factory closed had joined in the 1920s. A secure job meant the earth to people familiar with the deprivations of the Depression and war. As a morale booster, the BBC's 'Music While You Work' was allowed to be played on the radio. It was a live show, as all radio was back then.

The fear of people working in the West Midlands during World War II is seldom recorded, the focus falling on the razing of Coventry. One raid on BSA's factory, 15 miles (24km) north of Enfield's, resulted in the biggest single loss of life in a British factory during the war, yet nothing was reported beyond 'bombs fell on a West Midlands' town', because a government D notice prohibited it.

Redditch did suffer a number of bombings, the worst on the night of Wednesday, 11 December 1940. A German bomber followed a train heading to Redditch from

E. & H.P. Smith's purchase of Royal Enfield started well, with new investment promised and new models including this 175. BONHAMS

Conceived during 1961
and designed by the firm's
chief draughtsman, Reg
Thomas, Royal Enfield's
new lightweight model
first appeared in 1962.
This solitary prototype
was powered by a 173.5cc
engine that represented
a capacity class popular
in Continental Europe
and fell below the UK's
200cc limit that attracted
preferential insurance
rates. BONHAMS

Birmingham. When the train entered a tunnel in Redditch, the bomber veered off and dropped bombs on the town. It missed the factories but hit residential areas, killing six and injuring thirty-six. Glover Street was worst hit and many houses were destroyed by the bombs. The site is still known locally as 'the bomb site' and the old cemetery has the grave of a six-year-old child killed by the bombs. People would have been scared, but still they went to work. On their way they passed road blocks, trenches, flame fougasse (basically giant petrol bombs) and a Keep intended to serve as the final stronghold in the last stand against invaders. There were Bofors (fast-firing light anti-aircraft guns) and searchlights to defend against air attack. The Bofors guns were in place from 1939 until the end of the war. People could never forget how uncertain the future was.

But eventually peace returned and the post-war era brought more change. Finally what we would recognize as a production line appeared and a new canteen – 'messroom' – with kitchens was commissioned. Design and build were supervised by Francis W.B. Yorke FRIBA, and it was roundly criticized by many fellow architects as a brutal red brick modernist monstrosity. However, elsewhere it was lauded as 'proof of the progressiveness and modernity of the company that it would treat its workers so well'. It is also one of the best preserved of the Hewell Road factories, a few miles from what was the Royal Enfield social club, now converted

to apartments, and an old needle mill built in 1866, the oldest surviving building used by Royal Enfield and also in excellent condition, now used as offices. All are built with the distinctive local red brick – of course, this being Redditch clay – that people talk fondly of glowing in the evening sun.

The death of Major Smith in 1962, having effectively led the Royal Enfield family since the end of World War I, was a sea change. The new owner, E. & H.P. Smith, had originally been an electrical business, but via the stock market had expanded to become a holding company for twenty-five or so businesses, principally engineering manufacturers and suppliers in the Midlands. Initially all looked rosy, with fresh capital being promised and two men at the helm with motorcycle backgrounds, Leo Davenport from E. & H.P. Smith and Royal Enfield's own Major Vic Mountford. They had direct access to the directors of E. & H.P. Smith and liked ex-racer Davenport's idea of rekindling Royal Enfield's racing heritage. There were also new bicycles and the continuing development of the Interceptor, plus a new small trials bike, the Moto-X. This had a 250cc Villiers Starmaker engine and a respectable 22bhp, expected to be a big seller in the USA. It might have been, 1964 being the year that Hodaka started to sell such bikes to a hungry and booming off-road market in the USA, but sales of existing Royal Enfield models were falling dramatically and the GP5 was still a prototype when Major Mountford died in November 1964.

Major Mountford with K.R. Sundaram, director of Enfield India, in 1963.

1964

Geoff Duke O.B.E. *(FIVE TIMES WORLD CHAMPION)* rides Royal Enfield

Geoff Duke on the cover of the 1964 catalogue.

Having bought Royal Enfield for £800,000 and subsequently paying £2 million for Amalgamated Industries in the south of England, there were voices in E. & H.P. Smith arguing that Royal Enfield should be sold off – asset-stripped might be the term used today. With no one to argue Royal Enfield's corner the writing was on the wall. Acceptance by the US importers of a big price increase for 1966 meant that the Interceptor was removed from the home market and only three 350cc machines were offered, compared with over ten different models just three years before. In preparation for closing the Redditch works, Interceptor production was transferred entirely to the factories at Bradford-on-Avon.

As well as seeing the Interceptor leaving for Wiltshire, night watchmen were spending their time reading correspondence left on desks and soon the factory floor knew more than most of the management. The youngsters started leaving for nearby High Duty Alloys (HDA), part of Hawker Siddeley and making jet engine parts. Being heavily unionized, earnings at HDA could be twice those paid at Royal Enfield, but it was a trickier decision for older, long-term Royal Enfield employees who would forfeit their pension lump sum.

Another prototype, a 75cc two-stroke single. Chief draughtsman Reg Thomas wrote that it was tested with a five-speed Villiers-built engine and equipped with rubber block suspension. That machine had completed approximately 1,000 miles (1,600km) by the end of November 1963 and 'the 6-speed 75 or 98 and conventional rear springing [would have come] a couple of years later'. BONHAMS

The Royal Enfield social club between the wars. It is now apartments.

The float for the 1960 Redditch carnival.
ROYAL ENFIELD

Overhead camshafts were virtually unheard of in British motorcycles and certainly not in a 175. The cam's drive chain from the crankshaft's right-hand end, running inside a tunnel cast into the iron cylinder barrel, was topped by an alloy cylinder head. Aluminium castings extending rearwards contrived to make it look not unlike the Aermacchi Chimera. A new frame was complemented by cycle parts taken from other Enfield models, while the gearbox was a five-speed Albion unit. BONHAMS

To calm rattled nerves just before Christmas 1966, a large notice reassured staff that they should 'have no fears for your future employment – your future is assured. All members of staff will receive a £10 bonus for Christmas'. Within months machinery was being auctioned off at scrap value and Enfield Cycle Company – effectively now just a name – was sold to Norton Villiers/Manganese Bronze for £82,500.

It was the end of the road for the Redditch factories, if not for Royal Enfield. Many of the buildings were demolished when Redditch became a New Town in the 1970s and the industrial estate that was built in its place was named

Right-hand side of the Villiers-powered 75cc prototype from 1963. BONHAMS

the Enfield Industrial Estate. If you don't know what you're looking for, a huge slice of England's industrial heritage has simply vanished.

THE BRADFORD-ON-AVON WORKS

In June 1941, during World War II, part of the Royal Enfield Company moved from Redditch in Worcestershire to old underground stone workings at Westwood Quarry. In the safety of the quarry the firm carried out the manufacture of Type 3 predictor sights for anti-aircraft guns and control equipment for Bofors guns. As already noted, this underground facility at Bradford-on-Avon in Wiltshire was kept on after the war, together with many facilities for workers, some moved down from Redditch but most recruited locally. These people would not have needed the map of the surroundings of the Enfield Hostel, which detailed various 'beauty spots': each of them public houses.

When the war ended in 1945, Royal Enfield used the Bradford-on-Avon workers' engineering expertise to assemble motorcycles, initially from stocks of spare parts. The 250c Crusader, Meteor and Meteor Minor models

Royal Enfield printed a brochure illustrating their wartime efforts in the quarry mines around Bradford-on-Avon. A HERL INC

were made at Greenland Mills, Bradford, until 1963; the Interceptor was made at the former Wilkins Brewery in Newtown, Bradford, and at Westwood until 1970.

142

HORIZONTAL
BORING
MACHINE.

ASSEMBLING
35 c.c. ENGINES.

More from the Royal
Enfield leaflet illustrating
the Bradford-on-Avon
works; 35cc motors were
also made by Enfield
India.

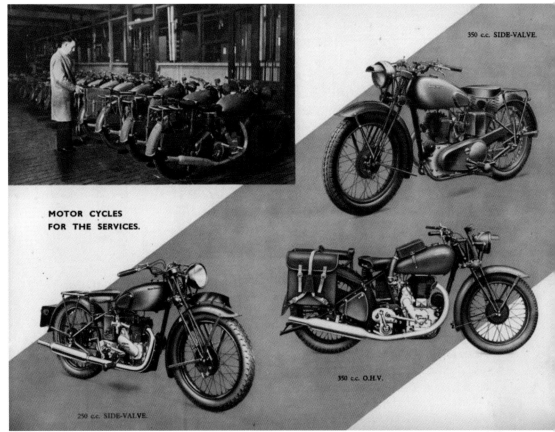

MOTOR CYCLES
FOR THE SERVICES.

350 c.c. SIDE-VALVE.

350 c.c. O.H.V.

250 c.c. SIDE-VALVE.

It is not generally
appreciated how many
motorcycles were built in
the Bradford mines during
the war.

A TEST RIDER'S TALE OF THE SERIES 2 INTERCEPTOR

You can usually find Richard Stevens' restored Series 2 Interceptor somewhere in his Devizes bike shop; either in the window, or out back in his workshop, ready to ride. When he bought his Royal Enfield it had been almost forty years since he'd ridden one, but in a way all Series 2 bikes are Richard's because, from 1967 until Enfield's demise in 1970, he was the Interceptor's development and test rider, based at Bradford-on-Avon. Royal Enfield was a latecomer to the parallel-twin party, arriving with the launch of the 1949 500 Twin. Almost immediately it was rendered obsolete in the all-important American market by the new BSA Golden Flash and Triumph Thunderbird 650s. Fortunately the 500's crankcases would take modified 350 Bullet cylinders, allowing engineer Tony Wilson-Jones to leapfrog the competition with the 693cc Meteor in 1953. This, and the follow-up Constellation, would be Britain's biggest parallel twins until the AMC/Norton 750s of 1962.

Wilson-Jones was clearly a chap who understood his American cousins and presumably had the stateside mantra 'there's no replacement for displacement' carved into his drawing board. So in 1963 his line of big twins sired the 736cc Series 1 Interceptor, the mightiest Enfield and a bike with so much torque that even later 750 British twins couldn't topple it for sheer twist and go, something for which American riders raised on big Harleys loved it. The Enfield's final ace was its legendary smoothness thanks to a massive one-piece iron crank, statically and dynamically balanced at the factory and running in two meaty main bearings. Alloy cylinder heads and con rods, twin 30mm Monobloc Amals and a choice of camshafts (three were offered) nailed the bike's performance colours to the mast, as did unashamedly stateside styling complete with a two into one exhaust. Designed from the outset for the US market, export Interceptors used a longer swinging arm for greater stability and wider handlebars. UK models gradually acquired most of these features and, with supply struggling to meet demand in America, the Interceptor was not even listed as a home-market model for 1966.

The Interceptor story coincides with a tumultuous period in Enfield's history. While the original Interceptor was developed and built at Enfield's Redditch works in the Midlands heart of the British bike empire, the Series 2 was developed at Enfield Precision Engineering at Bradford-on-Avon.

Having spent the war directly under the flightpath of Nazi bombers following the River Avon to Bristol, holding company Enfield Precision Engineering tucked itself away in a disused stone mine near Bath. After World War II, the company never got round to moving out of its cave and it was there that the lives of test rider Richard Stevens and the Interceptor first converged.

Richard is a Bradford-on-Avon boy, born and bred. He was completing his apprenticeship at a local garage when motorcycling friend Steve Hobbs, who worked at Enfield, suggested applying for the test rider's job he knew was coming up. 'I think a clean licence was my main qualification,' smiles Richard. He got the job and the unusual facilities didn't bother him: 'There was a long tunnel up from the workshop. We used to get a bollocking if we didn't keep our speed down riding the 500 yards to the surface. Apparently the noise was deafening if we gunned it.'

Developing the Series 2 meant being out in all weathers, piling on the miles before stripping the engine to see how improvements were holding up. Fellow test rider Dave Warner did the pre-delivery runs on a 15-mile (24km) circuit that meant he was easy to find if he went missing. 'Luckily I never had any real problems or crashes,' recalls Richard. The road riding required to evaluate tweaks was intense – up to 35,000 miles (56,315km) a year, running errands or just spinning the odometer. 'I loved the jumps below Westbury Hill; you could get airborne,' remembers Richard. 'The rain you got used to, and racing after a wet week – well, you could tell who had been out on a bike all week and who hadn't.' On trips to London Richard would wave at Tony Holland coming the other way, testing a Commando for Norton's Andover works. Visiting Birmingham, it would be Percy Tait racking up miles for Triumph who would get the nod.

To get the miles covered, Richard was often sent on long dispatches. One particular run to Wales sticks in his mind:

> I was sent to collect some switches. When I arrived they told me to take my van round the back where three huge boxes were waiting for me. Of course I wasn't in a van. We managed to strap two of the boxes to the pillion seat, they came up to my shoulders. Then we got one on the tank – getting on and off the bike was tricky.

As for riding kit, Richard has still got the pudding basin helmet he used to wear. In winter, even with a copy of the *Wiltshire*

Richard Stevens (left) on a Series 2 Interceptor racer c.1970, with Chris Ludgate on a Series 1. In suits are Reg Thomas and Roger Shuttleworth. RICHARD STEVENS' COLLECTION

Richard Stevens being photographed in his Devizes workshop for a feature in *Classic Bike* magazine.

Times stuffed down his jacket, he would still have to stop every 70 miles (113km) to warm up, gripping the exhaust pipes with his Barbour mitts. Even so, he was too cold to take them off at the end of the day, so his mum did it as he stood dripping on to the newspaper she'd lay out, ready for his return.

The Series 2 was a logical evolution, retaining the earlier bike's frame and rear hub, but updating the engine and front end. Lubrication was now wet sump with an oil cooler offered as an option. New Lucas ignition was specified and, crucially, the clutch was uprated on later bikes. Superior Norton forks also allowed an 8in (20cm) single leading shoe (SLS) drum to be fitted, a significant improvement over the Enfield drum on the earlier Interceptor. According to Richard: 'The original single leading shoe front brake's just terrible. If I could get some green linings for the one I have now that might help. Even with everything adjusted as it should be it's just not good enough, although the rear brake is a lot better.' Perhaps the reason the front brake was poor involved Royal Enfield's own original front forks. Richard adds that: 'The Norton forks were more rigid – you could bend the Enfield forks between your knees. The bigger brake was a lot better too.'

Richard worked on the Interceptor for three years. Not satisfied with living on the bike during the week, he persuaded the factory to let him race it at the weekends. He won a production series in 1969 on an Interceptor, *MCN* (*Motor Cycle News*, a UK weekly paper) making much of this, including a front-page splash showing two-time Daytona 200 winner 'Cal Rayborn trying out the new racer'. He was actually just riding around Heston Services car park; Richard had brought the bike up in a van and even had to lend international star Rayborn his riding kit.

Racing success meant that Richard was also busy systematically identifying weaknesses and helping the factory to solve them. Valve stem wear was an issue and the ancient four-speed gearbox was mated to a clutch that would seize in traffic. Richard remembers the clutch being a nightmare in London:

> *You'd be on the brakes and the bike would be running into the back of cars. Also, the primary chain would wear its guide – when you changed the oil, copper rivets and bits of nylon would come out. We developed a new guide. There were also problems with the tappet adjusters. Once there was an indent in the end of the valve it would rock as it moved, and wear the guide out, so we devised floating head tappet adjusters. It worked well on the development bike but didn't make produc-*

tion. But Porsche use a similar thing, and I've managed to get their parts to fit. Spot-on timing is also essential.

Richard's bike still retains its original points ignition, but 'Close attention to it keeps the engine running sweetly. The twin 30mm Amal Concentrics need to be set up properly too, but they're simple.' Richard also warned that the clutch is a weak point of the bike:

> *It drags pretty quickly if you're not on the open road. The very last bikes had a toothed clutch, more like a Japanese clutch, and they're better. The gearbox is one up, three down, and it doesn't like to be hurried. You can improve the action by taking a file to the ratchet mechanism; it shows you how in the workshop manual. Chris Ludgate, Enfield's chief design engineer, used to do that to my race bike, and polish the gears until they were like chrome, and it made a big difference.*

Enfield Precision Engineering's subterranean workshops are now out of bounds. Mining is occasionally under way again and the rooms that Richard remembers working in have been backfilled with rubble. With the factory gone, an Interceptor was the obvious touchstone to his years as a test rider. A friend dragged Richard along to an Enfield rally and there he heard of an American congressman with an Interceptor for sale in Washington DC. That deal fell through, but in 2008 Richard received an email from Canada with photographs of an apparently complete Interceptor for sale. He didn't waste any time: 'It took about four months to get it shipped over, and when it got here it all looked to be there; restored but never run. I've done nothing to it cosmetically, but I stripped the engine; it hadn't been put together terribly well but little needed replacing.' He also fitted indicators from an air-cooled RD Yamaha. The first time that Richard started the bike, memories came flooding back, though not particularly good ones. 'The clutch stuck – it was out of true,' explains Richard. 'Luckily it's an easy bike to work on; the gearbox just slides out like a cartridge.' The first ride was to an Enfield gathering in Gloucester to meet Andrew Stait, author of *The Mighty Interceptor*. Richard's bike was one of about twenty at the meeting and he found himself debating the bike's place in the pantheon of British greats:

> *I think the Bonneville was the better bike. It was the machine to have in production racing at the time.*

It was a better package, with good handling. And I remember people like Mick Andrew racing the Commando and having problems with flex thanks to the Isolastic engine mounts. The Interceptor deserved to outsell the Commando in the US – the Enfield had so much torque, American riders like that in a bike. And if we'd got the 800 into showrooms ... now that was really quick: 128mph; as fast as a Trident.

That's still a pretty respectable top speed for a production motorcycle; when the 800 Interceptor was being developed in 1969 it was phenomenal. And the figure's no urban myth, but the result of a legitimate timed run at MIRA, the UK's leading test facility. Ironically, it is now where Royal Enfield has its main overseas R&D facility and Richard has been a guest there, sampling the modern twins that we will come to.

Richard did much of the 800's development work in 1969 and felt that the bike was a huge improvement over the 750, although it still really needed a fifth gear and a better clutch. The revised styling was much racier, too. His most memorable ride on the 800 came when he gate-crashed a test day in which Triumph test pilot Percy Tait was putting a Trident through its paces. The 800 was as fast. 'Triumph's assembled staff did look surprised at our turn of speed,' grins Richard. 'Bit of an eye opener, I reckon.'

But after just a few months, the 800 Interceptor project was dead. In mid-1970, Norton-Villiers, owners of the Enfield marque, pulled the plug and the Bradford mine fell silent. Once it was all over for the Interceptor, Richard briefly worked in the Enfield fibreglass works, making aftermarket parts. He then returned to his original vocation as a mechanic for Holloway's in Bath, who'd recently moved on to Yamahas. The deal provided a Yamaha RD250 and TZ350 to race. Memorable successes included a fifth in the 1973 TT 250 production class and eighth on a Maico 125 when the TT was still a World Championship round. He also raced a Honda 400/4 in the F3 class of the legendary 1978 TT, although the con rods threw in the towel. The Yamaha connection continues today – Richard's been in his Devizes shop for over forty years. If you're ever in the area, pop in – you might get him talking about the best job in the world. 'I was paid to ride a bike,' he says. 'Unbelievable.'

The 800 prototype that Richard Stevens took to 128mph (206km/h) at MIRA, where he has recently tried the new Interceptor 650. HICTHCOCK'S MOTORCYCLES

ROYAL ENFIELD INTERCEPTOR SERIES 2, 1968–70 SPECIFICATION

Engine
Type: air-cooled parallel twin
Bore × stroke: 71 mm × 93mm
Capacity: 736cc
Compression ratio: 8:1
Carburettor: 2 × 30mm Amal Concentric
Fuel capacity: 2gal (9ltr) or 4gal (18ltr)

Transmission
Clutch: wet multi-plate gearbox four-speed

Brakes
Front: 8in drum
Rear: 7in drum

Suspension
Front: telescopic forks with hydraulic dampers
Rear: twin shocks
Chassis: frame single-loop tubular steel cradle
Tyres: front 3.50-19; rear 4.00-18
Wheels: spoked steel rims

Dimensions
Wheelbase: 57in (1,448mm)
Dry weight: 426lb (193kg)
Seat height: 31in (787mm)

Richard Stevens (right) in the entrance to the old Bradford-on-Avon works, part of a documentary made for the Indian factory.

OTHER VOICES REMEMBER ROYAL ENFIELD IN BRADFORD-ON-AVON

From 1967 to 1970, when the factory closed, the Royal Enfield Interceptors were assembled at Westwood and at Bobbin Lane from frames and parts made in the Midlands. Maurice Mumford worked there and is still friends with Interceptor test rider Richard Stevens, although he lives in Bath. They can both be found on the Royal Enfield Owners' Club stand at the annual Bristol Classic Bike Show. According to Maurice:

> *The factory was unique in being located in the underground stone quarry or mine. At its peak, it employed more than 600 people. After the war, the factory at Westwood made parts for the Royal Enfield motorcycles until the company's Redditch factory closed in*

1967. I really enjoyed the time I spent there. It was like working for one big happy family.

Derrick Elkins remained in Bradford-on-Avon, joining Royal Enfield as an apprentice during the late 1960s and working for them until 1970. 'It was brilliant. I used to love it. Eventually, I got to test-drive the Interceptor. It was a really comfy ride.'

The entrance to Westwood Quarry was below the houses – quarrymen's homes – of Upper Westwood. The stone that was quarried here, flecked with rusty patches, is still occasionally extracted when a match for a noteworthy building is required. As already noted, the underground quarry is now used as secure storage so is impossible to visit. Again, if you didn't know exactly what to look for there is nothing to suggest that not only some of Britain's motorcycling history lurks here, but that part of the war effort is also hidden away. If it wasn't for the motorcycles being built in India, it would seem as if Royal Enfield never existed.

11

NEW BEGINNINGS – THE INDIAN FACTORIES

A Bullet in India, with aftermarket cast wheels.

The first Prime Minister of India, Jawaharlal Nehru, tours the Enfield India plant in Chennai in the early 1950s.

It was the 1955 version of the 350 Bullet that was sent from the Redditch factory in kit form for assembly in India, the legacy of a 1952 order from the Indian Army for border patrol use. Royal Enfield's off-road reputation certainly helped to seal a deal with a country where rugged simplicity and reliability on unmade roads were highly valued. Enfield Bullets were originally supplied to the Indian military in 1953, going into service with the army on the borders with Pakistan, as useful at 18,000ft (5,500m) up in the Himalayas as in the deserts of Rajasthan.

However, the honeymoon period was short lived, as the newly independent government quickly decided that, while it liked the Bullet, a general policy of domestic manufacturing rather than importing goods should be adopted. Not one to look a gift horse in the mouth, Royal Enfield facilitated this with a joint venture to open a factory in Madras (now Chennai). Thus the 1955 model remained virtually unchanged in India despite the factory eventually building over 20,000 Bullets annually. Subsequent changes to the Redditch-built bikes were never incorporated by

the Indian arm, Madras Motors. The British and Indian lines diverged, never to meet again.

Initially, these Bullets had been shipped from England in 'knocked-down kit' form to be assembled in the Madras plant. A total of 163 Enfield India Bullets were completed by the end of the 1955, but Madras Motors quickly developed the facilities necessary to allow production of complete motorcycles under licence. A new factory at Tiruvottiyur, a few kilometres to the north of Madras, opened in 1956 to build Bullets under licence, initially with tinware and frames made in India, but with more complex items, including complete engines, still coming from England. These motorcycles' fuel tanks had 'Enfield India' alloy badges, with no identifying name at all on the engine cases, let alone the winged 'RE' so distinctively picked out in red on the British versions.

Madras Motors had a 51 per cent share in the new venture, with Enfield holding the remaining 49 per cent to comply with the Indian government's new legislation. Apprentices, including two sons of the new managing director, were shipped over to the Redditch works and began learning how the motorcycles were assembled. Eventually, Enfield sold much of the Redditch factory's tooling to Enfield India, there seeming little prospect of anyone in England's imploding motorcycle industry paying for them. But the Bullet suited India's roads and conditions well, and in the event of a breakdown it was easy to get fixed by one of the many small workshops that still exist in India. There were a few minor upgrades introduced over the coming years, but, even as late as 2007, you could still buy what was essentially a brand new 1950s' British bike, although since 1962 everything had been made in India and the Bullet had turned metric, starting with bearings in 1960.

Known as the 'Raja Gadi' (Royal Vehicle), the Enfield has become a status symbol for the simple reason that if you can afford one, you must be wealthy. The design has changed little over the years, as it is ideally suited to travel in India. The engine will run on fuel of just about any quality, the machine is immensely strong and can be ridden all day on appalling road surfaces in relative comfort – and with great economy. Break down anywhere and a mechanic will be a short walk away. Basic, infinitely repairable and invariably cherished, a Bullet will serve its owner almost indefinitely.

Many years ago I worked with an Indian Merchant Navy officer and as we approached the north-west coast of his homeland I asked what to expect. 'India is a very rich country with a lot of poor people,' he answered enigmatically, but it's true. The culture is breathtaking, but much of the poverty is heartbreaking and even a locally built Bullet is beyond the means of most. Yet the optimism and ambition of almost everybody you meet means that a Bullet is something many dream of owning one day. In the meantime, Enfield India needed to offer something people could afford and that something was the Fantabulus scooter introduced in 1962 with a Villiers two-stroke 7.4hp engine.

It was a commercial flop, but undeterred Enfield India introduced the 1963 Sherpa. Its 175cc two-stroke Villiers engine was again made under licence from Manganese Bronze, which already owned the engine builder. Incorporating a multi-plate clutch, four-speed gearbox and a robust and maintenance-free chain case, it was a surprisingly zesty baby Bullet. Front forks were Dowty units as fitted to the earlier British Ensign with rear shock absorbers from the Bullet. The toolboxes and the mudguards look disproportionately large for the otherwise petite Sherpa, but that's because they were in fact from the Bullet as well. This isn't surprising when the Sherpa had to be built to a price with minimal

investment. Royal Enfield was eager to entice young riders and those on a budget with small capacity two-stroke motorcycles and retain them in the hope that they might progress to a Bullet, which was by far the most expensive home-brewed motorcycle on the market.

The next project for Enfield India was the creation of an industrial engine division producing small 37cc engines for irrigation and this proved important both for the factory and Indian agriculture. The diminutive motors, produced in a plant in Thoraipakkam, 25 miles (40km) south of Madras, were vital in keeping the company afloat during a four-month strike and sit-in at the main Tiruvottiyur motorcycle plant near Chennai in 1966. By now, Enfield India was exporting to Australia, Nepal, Ceylon, Africa and the Middle East.

In 1970, the Sherpa was restyled and relaunched as the Crusader. Although the same Villiers engine was used, major changes included a bigger brake drum, front fork and headlight all from the Bullet; it started to be referred to as the 'mini-Bullet'. And then, in 1980, Enfield India released a new model actually called the Mini Bullet, with a 200cc two-stroke Villiers India engine. The model was intended as opposition to the Indo-Japanese two-strokes that were flooding the domestic market, but the Mini Bullet was not a success: its build quality was not a patch on the Japanese designs, even when they were built in India. The Enfield factory was dated compared to the purpose-built facilities in which the Japanese were investing.

BRITISH BIKES ARE COMING HOME – OR NOT

The above meant that what NVT did next was rather astonishing. By the time the 1970s arrived, the holding company owned pretty much all that was left of the British motorcycle industry, which amounted to an impressive roster of trademarks and a fractious relationship with the Triumph factory workers at Meriden. In the introduction to this book, an extract from December 1977's *Bike* magazine's test of the Enfield Indian Bullet quoted NVT chairman Dennis Poore observing that 'following an evaluation of the 350 Bullet no one seemed that keen [on importing it]'. NVT still owned a 30 per cent stake in Enfield's Indian outpost, so was keen to try to earn something from it. At the 1972 Earls Court Motorcycle Show, NVT therefore had Indian-built Crusaders on display, including one in full police regalia.

Enfields are so admired in India that if a male fashion model is to have any credibility he must have one on his billboard.

The company talked to the press about importing the Bullet alongside the Crusader, but quickly realized that there was no interest in either bike and no money to be made in motorcycling. There would be fits and starts as people paid to use various names, notably BSA on reimagined Yamaha trail bikes and big singles, but really it was the end of NVT. In 1973, the Triumph workers blockaded the Meriden factory and Manganese Bronze – which owned NVT – bought Carbodies, which designed, developed and built taxicabs, principally the iconic black London cab. Four wheels looked a lot less troublesome than two and NVT was eventually liquidated in 1978.

Meanwhile, at the 1977 Motorcycle Show Slater Brothers – already the UK Laverda importer – cheekily showed Bullets with fuel tanks repainted with 'Royal Enfield' scripts, rather than the 'Enfield India' alloy tank badges. There would be grumblings about who actually owned the rights to the Royal in Royal Enfield until the year 2000, because as we have seen it was used by Enfield Precision Engineering for Bradford-on-Avon bikes after the Enfield Cycle Company of Redditch had passed to NVT. Muddying the waters further was that Royal Enfield's spares business

Family transport, the Honda-based Hero.

had been sold to Velocette, which continued to use the Royal Enfield name and considered it theirs. And in the meantime, Enfield India and importers eventually started occasionally using the name, but given that these were still very basic motorcycles largely considered too troublesome to sell in any numbers outside of India nobody seemed to worry overmuch about who used the name. However, when the Eicher group took control in 1994 and set about turning Royal Enfield into a global brand, it also began registering names and trademarks, finally winning the right in UK courts to the Royal Enfield name by 2001.

We have already seen how dismissive *Bike* magazine was of the 1977 Enfield India (and badged as such), but the title was infamous for being deliberately provocative. *Motorcycle Mechanics* tried to be more balanced, yet even they concluded that the Bullet was 'a nice machine but really ought to be in a museum'.

Perhaps most damning was the report in *Motorcycle Sport*, which liked to see itself as the academia of the magazine world. Lengthy and thoughtful articles were clearly written by sages who felt that Japanese machines were a bit gaudy and real men need far fewer than four cylinders: 'How many letters have been published in the pages of *Motorcycle Sport* decrying the demise of the traditional British single? How many readers have said that they would buy one tomorrow if only it were still made? Now comes the chance to put their money where their mouth is.' However, like *Bike*, the tester hated the brakes and that the kick-starter did not fold in. Trying to come to terms with the lack of a steering lock, the writer suggested drilling holes in the yoke's head and using a padlock.

The author continued: 'It is difficult to decide whether we have been over-indulgent of the Enfield's faults in our delight at seeing a machine of such character back on the market.' Only being prepared to hint at reliability issues, the test concluded that the Bullet was 'Ideal for the two-bike man and the enthusiastic commuter, we would say, and fun too.' *Motorcycle Sport*'s readers did not buy one tomorrow as the tester had suggested; nor, indeed, at all. Yet the Bullet continued to trickle into the UK, finding popularity as a period lookalike sidecar outfit with Watsonian-Squire and Charnwood Classics. One even appeared in a Harry Potter film.

But Enfield India did not give up and in 1989 a new 24bhp 500cc Bullet was released, claiming to be aimed at export markets and available in Classic, Deluxe and Superstar trim. As financial and property markets crashed in much of the

No protective clothing, but astounding crash bars.

It's rare to see two Bullets away from the usual sea of scooters.

world, Enfield might have hoped that an economical, cheap motorcycle might find its time had come, but it was not to be. Motorcycles were now expected to be as unquestionably reliable as cars, even though the market was split between cheap commuters and the sports bike craze. The classic bike market was starting to gain traction as well, so Enfield was now competing with an industry that kept the real thing on the road. In truth, if you fancied an Enfield circa 1990 you could probably have a good Triumph Bonneville or a Norton Commando for the same sort of money. How times change.

Meanwhile, back in India, the protectionist nature of government policy meant that there was no serious competition from imported motorcycles, thus no need for improvement in the home market, and the Bullet struggled on essentially as a domestic commuter bike. However, eventually India opened up and the Japanese arrived in force, causing a downward spiral until, near bankruptcy, Enfield was bought by Eicher Motors, a tractor and commercial vehicle manufacturer, among other things. This was to be the making of a reborn Royal Enfield, and the start of a remarkable turnaround.

EICHER MOTORS TO THE RESCUE

India's population of almost a billion souls buys more than three million motorcycles a year, of which Enfield built just 25,000, all variations of the original Bullet. That needed to change if Enfield was to survive, never mind thrive. Under the newly appointed CEO of Enfield India, Siddhartha Lal, Eicher undertook major investment in the ailing firm and the company name was changed to Royal Enfield Motors. Many management and production changes were made, with the manufacturing process being streamlined and excess or outdated capacity closed. Without the large-scale government orders that had brought Enfield to India now bailing out the company, if the business was to become profitable the only option was selling to individuals via a dealer network.

And it did indeed all start to come right for Royal Enfield, both in sales and enormous value for shareholders. The credit is usually given to Siddhartha Lal, managing director and CEO of Eicher Motors. Success was eventually down to one bold decision that Lal took based on his love for Enfield, ironic in a world ruled by cold-hearted accountants. In 2004, Lal was just thirty when he inherited the top job at Eicher, with its diverse spread of some fifteen businesses including

tractors, trucks, motorcycles, components, footwear and clothing. But none was a market leader, so Lal decided to divest thirteen businesses and put all money and focus behind Royal Enfield and trucks, two businesses where he believed the group had a genuine shot at being number one in the field. 'In my mind the basic question was this: do we want to be a mediocre player in fifteen small businesses or just be good in one or two businesses,' recalled Lal in a 2017 interview with *The Economic Times of India*. 'I did the mathematics, projections and all we needed was to get the motorcycle business to the next level. I was clear that it would be an amazingly profitable business. But the company needed manufacturing scale. Fixed cost had to be spread around 100,000 bikes.'

Lal put his full weight behind Royal Enfield and the trucks business. A decade later, Royal Enfield was bringing in about 80 per cent of Eicher Motor's profits. Yet even by 2005, the company was still selling only some 25,000 bikes a year. Lal focused on Enfield first, leaving the trucks for later. He discovered how the bikes could be improved by riding hundreds of kilometres himself. He also initiated a motorcycling culture in the company, leading from the front by riding to work every day rather than using the company car.

Lal draws inspiration from global brands. Two of the examples he most admires are the Mini Cooper and Porsche, both of which are very focused and appreciate the importance of not diluting a brand's core DNA. When Lal was a student in the 1990s in the UK, small cars were designed to be cheap to build when compared to the mid-size and larger cars. Then came the Mini, which changed everything, showing that small cars could be well built, prestigious and fun to drive. 'That's what I want from Royal Enfield – to make middleweight motorcycles fun to drive, yet retain its DNA,' he said.

Royal Enfield exports jumped by 97.6 per cent by number, but actually fell as a proportion of production as Enfield reclaimed the booming home market. But Lal believed Royal Enfield could be a sizeable player in international markets as well as at home, so went head-hunting, ready to take on the world.

Rod Copes, a former Harley-Davidson manager, was hired as president of Royal Enfield North America; Pierre Terblanche, late of Ducati, was appointed head of the industrial design team; James Young, head of engines, had worked at Triumph and was hired in the UK. Simon Warburton, head of product planning and strategy (new projects), also came from Triumph. Mark Wells, head of programme (new projects) and Ian Wride worked on Enfield's Classic and Continental GT models while they were with the design firm Xenophya. Both joined Royal Enfield at its UK technical centre. Lal also realizes that good marketing is as important as fine engineering, which is why he recently hired Rudratej Singh from business giant Unilever. Singh joined as president in January 2015.

Royal Enfield announced its first takeover of another company in May 2015 with the purchase of UK motorcycle design and manufacturing stalwarts Harris Performance Products, which had already developed the chassis of the Royal Enfield Continental GT535. Harris works with the British-based part of Royal Enfield's development team, at the UK Technology Centre at Bruntingthorpe Proving Ground in Leicestershire. The team was established in January 2015 and moved into its new, purpose-built facility in May 2017. By the end of 2019, the team numbered 155 people and carries out a full range of design and development work, turning concept ideas into clay models, and from there hopefully to engineering design, prototyping and homologation.

The first Royal Enfield café in north Goa. It has a restaurant, clubhouse, museum and shop cum showroom.

Royal Enfield North America was established in 2015 under the nose of Harley-Davidson in Milwaukee, Wisconsin, the company's first direct distribution subsidiary outside of India. The initial intention was to offer three bikes, the Bullet 500, Classic 500 and Continental GT 535, believing this light–middleweight sector to be an underserved market. The dealership will be Royal Enfield's first company-owned showroom, a prestigious totem in the USA, according to Rod Copes. The company's intention is to establish some 100 dealerships in American cities, starting with Milwaukee. Royal Enfield is now selling motorcycles in more than fifty countries, having surpassed Harley's global unit sales in 2015.

In 2013, the company opened a new primary factory in the Chennai suburb of Oragadam on the strength of increased demand for its motorcycles. This was followed in 2017 by the inauguration of another new factory of a similar size to the facility at Oragadam (capacity 600,000 vehicles per year) at Vallam Vagadal. The original factory at Tiruvottiyur became secondary, but continues to produce some limited-run motorcycle models. Between them, the Indian factories now produce almost a million motorcycles a year; an impressive step change from the 25,000 being built when Lal took over.

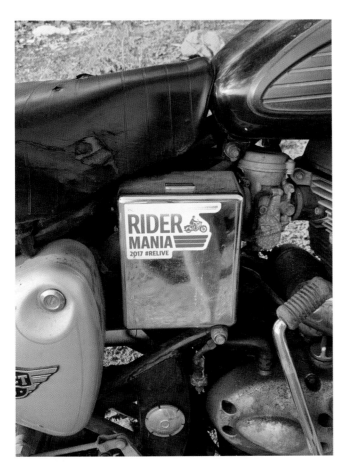

Rider Mania is another regular Royal Enfield event, gathering riders together as a family.

12

NEW HIT SINGLES

Royal Enfield and its Indian dealers actively encourage customization.

Publicity shot for the Himalayan tours. ROYAL ENFIELD

Having had a reputation as the bulletproof Bullet, by the 1980s doubts were creeping in. The factories were dated, tooling worn and customers' expectations had been completely reset by Japanese motorcycles. Most specifically, Royal Enfield was urgently in need of a motor that did not destroy its floating bush big end. The old cast-iron engine

had a piston-type oil pump circulating about 1ltr (1.8pt) of oil per minute at 5,500rpm, which is almost half of the Bullet's oil capacity, and led to overheating on India's modern highways. Speeds in the 1950s and 1960s were low as roads were often little more than dirt tracks, but now there were long stretches of metalled roads where the Bullet could be ridden flat out for long periods – until it broke down.

Eicher's takeover produced major advances in quality control, but design improvements were largely outsourced to European specialists. Swiss engineer Fritz Egli was a consultant to the factory for several years. British input continued with specialist Criterion involved in producing a new, five-speed gearbox to complement an electric-start Bullet.

156

Siddhartha Lal was as unsentimental about recruiting the best from overseas to improve the Bullet as he had been with finding people to work with him at the top of Royal Enfield. It was little surprise therefore that he chose AVL (Anstalt für Verbrennungskraftmaschinen List) to deliver him an all-new motor. AVL is an Austrian-based automotive consultancy as well as an independent research institute, employing over 11,000 people worldwide. AVL bills itself as the world's largest independent company for the development, simulation and testing of power-train systems.

Although AVL was charged with delivering an all-alloy lean-burn engine, it was to be designed as a drop-in replacement for the cast-iron original dating from 1955, so that the same chassis could be used with minimal disruption to production. The AVL update also brought a five-speed gearbox and fixed one of the long-standing quirks of the Bullet design – the gear shift is on the right, as it always was on British motorcycles, but still unusual and even illegal in some markets, most notably the USA. However, the new left-shift gearbox was not popular with Indian Bullet buyers, forcing the company to not only continue the Bullet Standard with the traditional four-speed layout, and even on the Electra it was offered only as an option. This led to the Electra four-speed (right-shift) and Electra five-speed (left-shift) variants, although the five-speed remained standard on all exports.

The first bike with this engine was launched in 1999 as the Bullet Machismo 350, but sales were disappointing. Prospective buyers not only hated the left-shift gearbox, but complained that it didn't sound the same as the old engine, lacking the distinctive thump of its predecessor. It also remained non-unit construction with a separate motor, gearbox and clutch, which, while it made putting it on to the production line simple, left it seeming old fashioned and prone to oil leaks while requiring oil to be changed and topped up in three different casings. This could hardly have seemed like progress, although the engine did better in the Thunderbird model, a chopper-style cruiser. This new motor came alongside the option of a front disc brake, but Royal Enfield struggled through the 1990s.

So all Royal Enfield engines, both the original cast-iron item and the new AVL lean-burn alloy units, still had three elements bolted together and retrospectively called the pre-unit construction engine. This complicated maintenance and also meant more gaskets and more potential leaks. AVL could clearly have handed Royal Enfield a unit-construction engine (designated UCE by Royal Enfield), but that would have meant retraining, new production techniques and a modified chassis. Lal was in a hurry and needed a stopgap motor while he built and modernized factories.

The AVL engine's biggest advantage was the ability to sit close to top speed for long spells without self-destructing. This was achieved with a roller big-end bearing and a gear-driven oil pump that delivered 2.42ltr (4.3pt) at 5,500 rpm – over double the old motor's capacity – and aluminium alloy castings, which dissipated heat better. However, the alloy also muffled sound less, making the AVL engines prone to valve-train clatter. This is one reason why a lot of Royal Enfield enthusiasts still preferred the cast-iron engine for its soulful thump, even though the AVL engine was far superior.

The company also faced the difficult task of catering to a very diverse market. To preserve the Bullet's nature and reputation as a classic British bike and to attract youngsters away from the performance motorcycle market, the Bullet marque was split into two. The Bullet Standard 350 featured all of the increased manufacturing quality and reliability, but maintained the traditional Bullet look and was available only in black. A new model, available in more colours and with chrome detailing, CDI electronic ignition and gas-filled rear shock absorbers – but with the same engine and gearbox as the Standard – was launched. This model was called the Bullet Electra and the 350 went on to become the bestselling Royal Enfield model, accounting for around half of the company's sales.

A DIESEL DIVERSION

While a British initiative had created the first Diesel Enfield, the Robin, powered by a Fuji single-cylinder motor usually used as a generator, as well as supplying complete chassis for the Robin, Enfield India ran with the idea. Speaking to the British press just after the Eicher buy out, the export manager was embarrassed to admit that it was still in the range despite what he admitted were the diesel's limitations.

It can only achieve 0–60mph in 23 seconds, but returns 190mpg. Top speed is limited to 65mph, but our production of 300 a week was only aimed at small domestic urban commuting applications. Speed and acceleration in this area are academic as economy and flexibility are of greater importance to our customers.

With its improved fuel consumption, the lean-burn 350 AVL motor was intended to make the diesel obsolete, going into production for the Indian market in a new factory in the northern desert city of Jaipur. But despite initial resistance in the home market – and the closure of the Jaipur factory in 2002 – in the long term its UCE follow-up fared better than BMW's attempt to break into one of the world's biggest markets with an F650 manufacturing operation. The Germans left with their tails between their legs, as did Kawasaki, who abandoned their joint manufacturing and import agreement with Bajaj Auto in 2017.

Enfield India on the other hand not only learned what its domestic customers valued, but also had a clear understanding of its export markets, which at the Eicher takeover represented more than 10 per cent of production. Its outgoing director, Pravin Purang, claimed in 2001:

We export all over Europe, the US and Canada and receive great numbers of inquiries from Japan. They've produced some of the best bikes ever made, *but are seeking nostalgia. That is really where we score, in the export leisure markets, even the hobby market. We sell bikes to customers who would really like a vintage machine, but don't want the pain and trouble of owning one. The intention of our development work is to produce an original, classic machine on the outside, with modern, more reliable internals, capable of complying with emission laws in the major export markets.*

FINALLY, A UNIT-CONSTRUCTION ENGINE

What Enfield needed was an all-new motor and realistically it had to be a unit-construction engine, or UCE as Royal Enfield referred to the project. One of the other things rarely considered in the unit versus non-unit debate is getting the engine's power to the rear tyre. Both the cast-iron and AVL 350cc motors made 18bhp at the crank, but this

Bullet for hire – £8 a day.

The Trails Bullet.

dropped to 12bhp at the rear wheel, a whopping third of the power made lost to the transmission. The new UCE 350cc engine claimed 19.8bhp at the crankshaft and 16bhp at the rear wheel; still a 20 per cent loss, which is a lot for a modern motorcycle, but acceptable to Royal Enfield for a simple low revving, big single. The UCE was also more fuel efficient than both the cast-iron and the AVL lean-burn engines by almost 20 per cent. A faster-cooling alloy cylinder, stronger crankshaft and con rod, improved oiling, twin spark plugs and a host of other features were all part of the new engine. To further reduce maintenance, there were hydraulic valve lifters instead of solid tappets acting on the pushrods, as the latter required regular adjustment. Instead, the UCE uses pressurized oil to drive the push-rods. giving more consistent performance and claimed to be good for at least 12,500 miles (20,000km) before need-ing any kind of attention.

The UCE replaced the seventy-year-old Royal Enfield cast-iron engine, which had the – possibly dubious – distinc-tion of being in production longer than any other motor-cycle engine in history. Production ended in 2008 with the arrival of the UCE. There was then an even bigger step change when the 500 UCE was originally unveiled at 2008 motorcycle shows in Cologne, Germany, and Birmingham, England, specifically aimed at export markets, although it took until a few years later for the new units to reach the USA. The new single-cylinder 500cc unit brought elec-tronic fuel injection (EFI), rather than the 350's lean-burn Mikuni CV carburettor.

A US tester liked the lazy nature and the lowly rpm at which the peak power was delivered, making for a very commuter-friendly experience through slow-moving traf-fic, with the bike pulling with aplomb in low revs and high gears. The engine felt substantially refined when compared with its predecessor and transmits just the right amount of vibration to the handlebars. It was important that US riders liked the 500, because this was the first motorcycle manufactured in India that could be sold in the USA as DOT (Department of Transport) approved and Euro-3 compliant.

Inevitably, however, first deliveries were at home, with the cruiser-style 2008 Thunderbird Twinspark. The retro-styled Classic version was initially reserved for export, but when launched in India in 2009 it immediately achieved cult

status and sales grew rapidly. As the reputation for much-improved quality spread, demand improved as well and by 2010 the company was selling 50,000 bikes a year, but on three platforms or base models. Lal decided to build all Enfield bikes on a single platform to maximize economies of scale. The Enfield Classic, launched from this single platform, helped sales to increase six-fold in half a decade to 589,293 in 2014.

To get to that number, the Tiruvottiyur plant set a new production record of 113,000 motorcycles built in 2012. The following year work started on a new factory in Oragadam, an industrial suburb of Chennai, 36 miles (58km) south-west of the city centre. It had excellent communications, ready to supply Eicher's export ambitions. The state of the art factory even includes a robotic paint facility and is a world away from the factories that Eicher originally inherited.

GT Continental 535 casually parked by the side of the road in 2017, at the time probably the most expensive motorcycle in India.

An early production line; the Eicher transformation has been remarkable. ROYAL ENFIELD

Remarkably, no additional security seems to be needed in India beyond an ignition key.

JOIN THE CLUB –
GETTING EXCLUSIVE

In truth, while the Royal Enfield singles have a certain old-world charm, they were not particularly good motorcycles. Certainly they have a fabulously loyal customer base at home, but overseas they are a curiosity. With the Chinese gearing up with bargain basement copies of Japanese motorcycles and the vast majority of motorcycles sold new in the West being on personal contract purchases (PCPs), a low price alone would never be enough. A retro such as the Triumph Bonneville or Kawasaki W650 (later 800) costs not much more, a few pounds a week on a PCP. If you just wanted a motorcycle, the much admired Yamaha MT-07 was pretty much the same price as the range-topping Royal Enfield singles. So the real challenge is to make people want – really want – a particular motorcycle.

The man who wrote the book on doing this is Federico Minoli, a charming, dapper Italian who built a reputation in the USA for being a turnaround specialist, notably with Unilever. But he's also a motorcycle enthusiast, so when the Texas Pacific Group bought Ducati in 1996 they called in Minoli. Ducati had iconic models – the 916 and the Monster – but were really a niche player only selling to true enthusiasts who put up with any number of issues, including taking flak from riders of Japanese bikes who couldn't grasp why people would pay a premium for a product that was expensive to run, even if you could afford to buy one, and was prone to breaking down.

But Minoli understood why some of us felt that way and set about teaching everybody else. Like Eicher, he knew quality had to improve. But he understood that Ducati riders were a loyal band, both to each other and to the factory, so he set about expanding how that might work. Instead of motorcycles, marketing and advertising material featured Ducati people – not a random test rider, but someone who owned a Ducati or worked in the factory. He created the World Ducati Weekend and reinvented the Motogiro d'Italia as a five-day ride across Italy. I was lucky enough to meet Minoli on his final Motogiro, just before he left Ducati, but don't think that affects my judgment. In just five years, revenues quadrupled and Ducati's market share of the sports bike sector had increased by more than 30 per cent. Minoli's work at Ducati is now celebrated as an example of a successful corporate turnaround through

managerial focus, and pre-MBA reading can include a 2002 Harvard Business School case study that documented the remarkable transformation of Ducati under his leadership.

Minoli's transformation of Ducati was because he had a singular understanding of Ducati's business. They were not a metalworking, mechanical or even a motorcycle company. They were an entertainment company with motorcycles at their heart. They could not compete in manufacturing efficiency, but they could excel in creating a community that built on Ducati's history.

You can't help but wonder if Siddhartha Lal has read the case study. Since 2011 Royal Enfield riders around the world are encouraged to join in a 'One Ride' event, taking place on each first Sunday in April. A factory organized trip crosses the Nepalese border for the first time with 'Tour of Nepal' and tours of the Himalayas are turned into a major event.

Then in 2014 Royal Enfield introduced a new retail experience in India with the opening of an exclusive clothing store at Khan Market, New Delhi, which was soon rolled out globally. In 2017, the company opened its first café, the Royal Enfield Garage Café, in Baga, Goa. When I visited there were two other British couples there, one hiring a Bullet for a week's travel. The daily rate was barely half what a taxi would cost and you have to pay for your own fuel. But touring India on a Royal Enfield? That's the experience of a lifetime.

When you visit the Royal Enfield website you are first shown the 'Made Like a Gun' icon, then a rider on a motorcycle, then a compass with a wandering dotted line, all before a page loads. The message is clear – get out there and be part of a tradition, and go on a ride, ideally an adventure.

A friend rode the Himalayas tour on a 350 Bullet and told tall tales of the bike's indestructibility and images of the trip are never far from his social media posts. He bought a Turbo Twin to remind him of his residual affection for Royal Enfield. Another friend – I'm lucky enough to have several – bought a 410cc Himalayan and declared it the best motorcycle for solo riding he'd ever owned, having started his motorcycling career on a Royal Enfield Continental GT 250. Ironically for someone whose first motorcycle came with clip-ons, he never disappeared down the sports bike rabbit hole that most of us inhabited during the 1990s and 2000s, instead putting in many miles two-up touring on big

The modern Trail version of the Bullet with its
counterpart the Himalayan in the foreground.

Moto Guzzi V-twins. But now he wonders if those mighty Mandello del Lario masters of mileage might be too heavy and is contemplating a trade-in for a new Interceptor. It seems that if you're in the market for the simple pleasures of motorcycling a visit to a Royal Enfield showroom is now as good a place to start as any. Affordable, handsome and unintimidating, but with a sense of history underscored by a name recognized by most.

In 2016, Royal Enfield debuted the Himalayan, its first adventure motorcycle. With an all-new 411cc single over-head cam (sohc) engine and long-reach suspension, it was designed to give adventurous riders the right tool for all roads and no roads. In truth, it's noisy and slow away from back roads, if vibration-free, and 24.5bhp sometimes isn't enough on a busy motorway. But it offers great value even if the alloy panniers add over 10 per cent to the price and, like the other Royal Enfield singles, it's non-threatening, charming and engaging – and very affordable.

As proof that the love for Royal Enfield is still growing, in 2018 the Royal Enfield Classic 500 Pegasus, a homage to the WWII Flying Flea, was launched at the Imperial War Museum, Duxford. Limited to just 1,000 individually numbered motorcycles worldwide, the Indian market allocation of 250 machines sold in less than three minutes.

Publicity shot for the
Himalayan model.
ROYAL ENFIELD

THE 500 SINGLE IS DEAD – LONG LIVE THE 350

Royal Enfield announced in early 2020 that it is drawing a line under production of the long-lived 499cc single-cylinder machines in the face of strict new Bharat Stage VI emissions limits in India – equivalent to Euro 5 – but the company is preparing to replace them with completely redesigned 349cc singles all over the world.

The updated 350 models had been regularly spied undergoing testing in India and, while Royal Enfield has traditionally not bothered with the 350 in Europe, opting instead to sell its 500 range, it has now type-approved a Euro 5-compliant range of 350s for sale. After all, anyone wanting anything bigger now has the option of the 650 twin.

As well as the Bullet 350 and Classic 350 – which will seem familiar, since it looks much like the existing Bullet 500 and Classic 500 – Royal Enfield has also type-approved a Meteor 350. It was clear that Royal Enfield planned to revive the Meteor name in 2019 after the firm registered a trademark on the moniker. At the time, it seemed likely that the name would be used on a derivative of the new twin-cylinder 650cc models, it having originally been used on a 700cc twin.

The Meteor 350 looks like the Thunderbird 350 that is sold in India, with a 20mm longer wheelbase than the Bullet or Classic, as well as wider, taller bars. Royal Enfield can't use the Thunderbird name in Europe, since Triumph has the trademark rights on the name and Ford owns it elsewhere. For the same reason, the cruiser is currently known as the Rumbler in Australia.

All versions of the new 350 make just shy of 20bhp, which is almost 30 per cent down on the outgoing 499cc models. The new engine is also rather higher-revving that the outgoing version, with peak power coming at 6,100rpm rather than the 5,350rpm of the old model. Ready to ride, the Bullet and Classic 350s will come in at 193kg (426lb), while the Meteor 350 is 191kg (421lb).

Finally, a mention of the beautiful but flawed Continental GT 535. Launched in 2013, it was the first Royal Enfield to feature a frame designed by UK-based Harris Performance, now owned by Royal Enfield. The Continental GT impressed with surprisingly good handling and braking, but the big single could not offer the kind of performance to match the chassis and it also suffered from vibration at higher revs. There were a few quality issues and the price was high by Royal Enfield standards, meaning that the GT was adored by a few, but never sold in the hoped-for numbers. Once the 650 twins were on the way it was quietly dropped.

If Royal Enfield's singles needed to be cheap and cheerful to sell outside of India, the company's marketing folk had no problem getting the cheerful side sorted. Images of the bikes being ridden along the beach with a surfboard strapped to the side abound. Happy youngsters around a bonfire – in Royal Enfield apparel, of course – are photographed with Bullets and Classics lurking in the background. I'm less sure about the Himalayan splashing through a stream in a scene that's dangerously close to a BMW GS pastiche, but when you look at the price list you might well be tempted. For the price of a big Beemer you could fly to India, buy a Himalayan, ride it home and still have enough money left over to buy a Bullet.

But as someone lucky enough to have owned a Ducati 450 Desmo – now a fifty-year-old single-cylinder motorcycle – the Royal Enfield singles have always underwhelmed. Admittedly the 450 Desmo is now priced at collector's silly money, but not so long ago its non-Desmo 350 sibling could be had for the price of an Enfield. I could never see why you'd choose the Enfield, which still looked and performed like something from another age and was built down to a price. With the GT535 I could see the attraction, Siddhartha Lal clearly no longer content to rely on Royal Enfield's enormous domestic market, where its rustic, old-school single has been a hugely popular workhorse for the past half-century. The company is now targeting growth through export sales, starting with the Continental GT, launched to a huge fanfare at the Ace Café in London and having invited what looked like the whole world's motorcycling press. But then the road tests arrived, *Bike* magazine making risqué comparisons to Ann Summer's product range and highlighting the price. No wonder it couldn't be sold alongside the 650 – it was just a few hundred pounds less than the new entry-level twin and that had over 50 per cent more power. If Royal Enfield wanted to export in large numbers they finally had the bike for the job.

13

THE NEW TWINS

Chrome tank version of the new 650 Interceptor.

An original Royal Enfield twin in the mini-museum.

I bumped into Richard Stevens at the Bristol Classic Bike Show. We exchanged pleasantries and, knowing he'd been invited up to MIRA, I asked if he'd had a ride on the new Interceptor. Of course he had. 'Lovely bike, so much lighter than mine.' Though in fact it isn't, Richard's bike being 193kg (426lb) versus the new bike's 202kg (445lb); the new bike just feels it with lighter controls and compact dimensions. He continued: 'Just a lovely bike. And how much is it? Under six grand?' I nod. And then smile as he uses the same word with which he finished his story about being paid to ride a bike: 'Unbelievable.'

And it is. The basic Ducati Scrambler is 15 per cent more, many built in Thailand. The Triumph Bonneville is also made there, yet costs 50 per cent more than an Interceptor.

Everything changed with the 650 Interceptor and its sportier cousin, the Continental GT 650. While the Interceptor will quite certainly prove to be more popular thanks to its upright seating position, the Continental GT 650 brings café racer kudos to the range. The air-cooled 648cc engine uses a 4-valve head – an Enfield first on a road bike – and promises a healthy 47bhp. Royal Enfield's 650 (the Interceptor name is owned by Honda in the USA, so it's dubbed the INT 650 there) is the company's first twin-cylinder motorcycle in over fifty years.

Emphasizing the significance of the new 650 twins, Siddhartha Lal confirmed at the international press launch in Santa Cruz, California, that the project is 'the biggest and most important in my career'. It is possibly actually the most important moment in Royal Enfield's illustrious history, 'a company with UK roots, an Indian soul and a global approach,' according to Lal.

The new 650 Royal Enfield Interceptor and Continental GT twins were unveiled at the 2017 EICMA Motorcycle Show in Milan, Italy, and at Rider Mania in Goa, India. The first thing to note for an all-new motor designed to be sold in Europe and the USA is that it's air-cooled. Triumph has given up on that, despite the fact that it rather kills the retro look for many: after all, it's impossible to mistake a retro for a genuine classic when there's a big radiator and water pipes on display. The Royal Enfield 650 motor is a handsome hunk of polished alloy that manages to look like the original Interceptor and modern at the same time. A single overhead cam kept it looking as if it might have pushrods while coping with 4 valves per cylinder. The view from the saddle is impressive at any price point, the dials spared the scars of digital displays, although the bolted-on cross brace is slightly odd. There are metal mudguards and a general lack of plastic.

Walking around the bike you'd never guess the price and perhaps you wouldn't guess it's brand new. Start it up though, and the 270-degree crank immediately gives the game away. Originally, British twins used a 360-degree (that is, firing once a revolution) crank, since this made running with a single carburettor straightforward. The Japanese twins used 180-degree cranks to minimize vibration, even if it meant that two carburettors were needed. And then Yamaha came along with the TRX aimed at Ducati's cam-belt 900SS that used a 270-degree crank to give a parallel-twin motor the drive and sound of a V-twin. Since then, Triumph has used the idea, which is why some of us are forever expecting to see a Ducati, and then disappointed with a Triumph. And now Royal Enfield is in on the act. Apparently 180- and 360-degree versions were tested, but the decision to install the 270 architecture was unanimous among test riders. A counter-balancing shaft eliminates a large proportion of the vibration, but there remains enough for the motor's character to shine through.

The motor makes 47bhp, albeit not until 7,250rpm, although crucially the bhp figure equates to 35kW, which in turn means that an A2-licence holder (that is, riders who have yet to pass a final test or reach a certain age) can enjoy

Now that's a proper tank badge if you hate stickers.

The red and black colour scheme is very like Coventry Eagle's post-war look. ROYAL ENFIELD

The chrome tank version looks most like the Interceptor Series 1. ROYAL ENFIELD

the Interceptor. Cruising along at 70mph (113km/h) in sixth gear – another first for Royal Enfield – and the bike will be ticking along nicely at just under 4,000rpm, although over-taking will need some down changing. There is a lightweight slipper clutch, an emphatically brilliant throttle response and a torquey feel, with 80 per cent of the torque available at 2,500rpm.

The overall feel of the engine, from the sound to the fuel-ling, throttle action, seamless power delivery and beyond is impressive given the price of the bike. The 650 is a chance to kill any previous reputation Royal Enfield had for poor quality or unreliability and riders' forums are full of five-star reviews, only the occasional electrical problem causing concern. It is a remarkable leap forward, proving Eicher's massive invest-ment in a new factory with multimillion pound research and development centres in Chennai and Harris Performance at MIRA, both with deep pools of talent. They've created a brand-new classic bike with all the qualities of a modern-day

machine. A 1,007-point check taking six hours each time a bike is rolled off the production line is claimed, called a 'maturity process' by Enfield. This post-production check focuses on every detail from indicator alignment to ensuring that the wiring loom isn't chafing anywhere. A three-year unlimited mileage warranty backs this up.

For a bike with such a low price point there had to be compromises, but there were corners that could not be cut. Test riders insisted on the Pirelli Phantoms; the front is a standard tyre, but the rear is a bespoke 130/70-18, which might cut down on aftermarket options. The chassis is clearly a relative of the Continental GT 535 and again devel-oped by Harris Performance. A sturdy cradle-type structure allows for a degree of rigidity. A single 320mm disc on the front is gripped by a twin-piston ByBre (Brembo's budget range) and a dual-channel Bosch ABS system is just enough to halt this 202kg (dry) motorcycle well enough. A second disc isn't an option.

THE CONTINENTAL GT 650 – SAFE-DANGEROUS

Mark Wells, head of programme (new projects), says that this was about creating a machine that is a simple joy, and it is. Finally it's the motorcycle that the GT 535 was meant to be, a café racer for the modern age. While the promotional video for the Interceptor very much revolves around the Californian dream – beaches, sunshine and canyons – the GT 650 imagery is around London's cool east end, home to the Bike Shed, although it's not shown. Road testers complaining that the clip-ons are less comfortable than the Interceptor's handlebars seem to be missing the point; owners seem happy to trade comfort for the café racer aesthetic and at least

The white colourway for the **Continental GT 650** is unusual. ROYAL ENFIELD

A Royal Enfield is at home in India and England, and has been for almost seventy years. ROYAL ENFIELD

the footrests are set further back than the Interceptor's. The complaint that the sporty riding position just emphasizes the budget suspension, brake and modest power again is something that doesn't bother those who paid for their Continental one jot. Indeed, owners who have had – or still have – a big Japanese sports bike seem to relish a motorcycle that encourages you simply to pull on a leather jacket and helmet and just ride.

Anthony – Dutch to everyone – van Someren is founder and CEO of the Bike Shed Motorcycle Club. It started as a blog and rapidly turned into a show – the first one was free, the second a fiver to get into and most exhibitors still didn't have to pay to be there, which is how I met Dutch and spoke to him about the concept. We had both disappeared down the sports bike rabbit hole – he on KTMs, me on Ducatis – and realized that it meant getting up unfeasibly early on a Sunday morning so that you could enjoy your motorcycle as the designer intended. My way out became classic bikes, rekindling a love for the motorcycles I'd loved as a teenager. Dutch, being rather younger than me, had a very different epiphany. A friend who was a latecomer to motorcycling bought a Bonneville to learn to ride on – a strange phrase to those of us who came to motorcycling in an age when what you learned on was first limited to 250cc – and kitted himself out in the sort of fashion the original Bonneville riders might have done. Dutch turned up to meet him outside a café on a big KTM in one-piece armoured leathers that – like my old ones – are almost impossible to walk or stand straight in. The friend couldn't believe how many strangers approached him to ask about the Triumph, while women would ask about his jacket. The KTM, worth the best part of three times the Bonneville's price tag, went unnoticed. On being told this, I observed that my Ducati Monster always brought out the pester power in people, while I was left alone with my 916 series bikes.

The truth is that it wasn't just sports bike riders who had lost their way, it was the entire motorcycle industry. Egged on by magazine testers forever, Oliver style, asking for more, bike factories offered machines that could run at race pace on a track day, or carry you around the world. Even Ducati seemed to be forgetting – in the words of Federico Minoli – that they were an entertainment company with motorcycles at their heart. A few people for a few years might relish a big sports bike, but even they would probably concede that riding one is exhilarating rather than entertaining. And most people are probably right to be intimidated by a motorcycle that makes well over 100bhp.

Dutch called the appeal of the Bonneville safe-dangerous. You need a helmet, but not one that intimidates, Darth Vader style. You need protective clothing, such as heavyweight jeans and a stylish jacket, but can do without knee sliders and aerodynamic humps. Safe-dangerous is something outsiders can imagine trying – surfing, amusement park rides, a parachute jump – rather than something than needs years of experience and a certain level of talent. Something inclusive rather than excluding. As Mark Wells put it, a simple joy.

So Dutch and his team opened the Bike Shed in Shoreditch and while the big screen shows MotoGP races live, the old railway arch that is its home has a laid-back, old-world feel that is clearly home to motorcycle enthusiasts while being welcoming and unintimidating. Bikes come and go, but last time I was there, there was a group of twenty-something girlfriends in party frocks enjoying cocktails and a middle-aged couple – he in a tailored pink shirt – enjoying lunch. You wouldn't see that at the Ace Café.

Take a Bullet at the café.

The black and gold **Continental GT 650** is very much a classic look. ROYAL ENFIELD

The bar at the café, complete with the inner workings of an Enfield.

This montage is made up of old books in the clubhouse.

I remembered this when I visited the Royal Enfield Café in Goa in January 2020. There was an Interceptor and a Continental GT 650 parked outside, as well as old singles and a row of scooters. Most impressive were the customized bikes, something Royal Enfield is keen to promote. A while

These traditional looking Goan tiles reflect the Portuguese heritage, but look closely and they are bespoke to the Royal Enfield Café.

back, I observed that the price of the Himalayan was such that you could fly to India, buy one to ride home and have change. At the mini museum by the café was a Himalayan modified for shale racing, but also outside were a handful of customized bikes. The 650 twins especially offer such value for money that you could instead spend the savings over the equivalent machine from other manufacturers by personalizing your very own Interceptor or GT 650. Royal Enfield is keen to promote this idea.

These ingredients might just save motorcycling itself. While the average age of most motorcycle buyers now hovers uncomfortably around fifty years old, in India buyers of brand-new Royal Enfields are just twenty-seven. And, as you'd expect from youngsters, their bikes get customized, ridden at speed, to the beach and into the mountains. There's a joyous motorcycling culture around Royal Enfields in India that's more like the West's in the 1960s and 1970s, where we

seem to have adopted various po-faced values based around originality or covering high mileages. Yet here's the thing: while most histories of Royal Enfield view the Indian connection as little more than a footnote, in truth it's a vibrant link to a future that will soon see India having been home to Royal Enfield motorcycles for longer than England ever was. Royal Enfield bolted together motorcycles in a green and pleasant land between 1901 and 1970: sixty-nine years. India might have started late – 1955 – but 2025 will mark the seventieth anniversary of Royal Enfield's eastern adventures.

As already noted, the 650 twins will make an excellent base for the custom houses that are taking off across the world. London's Malle, a premium motorcycle clothing and luggage manufacturer, has already been showing off two customized Interceptor 650s, which look simply stunning. And in a very different shade of customization, Cayla Riva, an eighteen-year-old racer from California, set a new land speed record of 157.053mph (252.752km/h) during the 2018 Speed Week at the Bonneville Salts Flats. Her bike, a Continental GT 650 twin, was specially prepared for Bonneville with S&S Cycle engine tuning and a Harris Performance frame.

Rounding up, Royal Enfield's bet on the 650 twin seems to have paid off thanks to an engaging motor, classic looks erring on the side of simplicity and just enough nostalgic history. Royal Enfield has no doubt ruffled some feathers in the Triumph and Harley-Davidson camps, and they're not finished yet.

ROYAL ENFIELD INTERCEPTOR SPECIFICATION

Engine
Type: air-cooled parallel twin
Bore × stroke: 78 × 67.8mm
Capacity: 648cc
Max. power: 47bhp at 7,250rpm
Fuel capacity: 13.7ltr (3gal)

Transmission
Gearbox: six-speed
Clutch: wet multi-plate

Brakes
Front: 320mm disc
Rear: 240mm disc

Dimensions
Wheelbase: 1,400mm
Dry weight: 202kg (445lb)

BACK TO THE FUTURE – ANOTHER V-TWIN?

That Royal Enfield surpassed Harley-Davidson's global sales in 2015 has already been noted, but that was by units rather than value. With Royal Enfield's most expensive model costing less than Harley's cheapest, there's still enormous room for improvement outside India. Especially if you could offer a bobber V-twin that cheekily takes the Harley Sportster's historic 883cc capacity and uses it to repackage your own heritage.

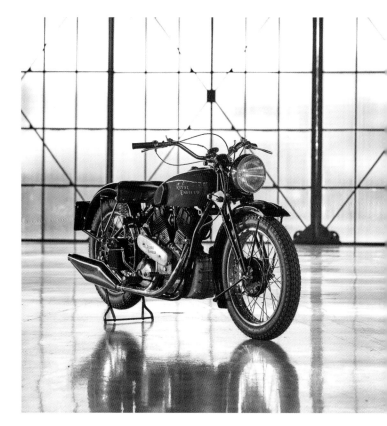

An original Royal Enfield V-twin – is a new one on the way? ROYAL ENFIELD

'Of all the models in Enfield's history the KX is my favourite,' said Siddhartha Lal, after Royal Enfield stunned the world at the 2018 Milan show by unveiling the Concept KX bobber – a modern reimagining of a 1930s Royal Enfield model. The original KX was an air-cooled side-valve V-twin with a monstrous 1140cc displacement. Lal explained that: 'It's from such a fascinating time in motorcycling history. It was before the English and American markets split into parallel twins and cruisers, so it has style elements that we would associate with both. My personal favourite part is the tank; there are no other shapes like it out there.'

The Concept KX apparently originally started life as two new machines, but the finished thing is a perfect combination of modern and classic styling cues. The modern swooping girder fork with integrated headlight and nacelle is the perfect reimagining of the front end on the classic machine. The pancake-style exhaust, single seat unit and flat tank also faithfully modernize the original KX, while Enfield's job of hiding all the electronics is a master stroke. Lal continued:

It's good to give the team something to do without the restraints of a production bike. I told them I like this one, then it was just a case of giving them the time and the budget. The work they have done is amazing; it went from idea to finished concept in less than six months. We actually drew up a few different designs that ranged from very classic tributes to the KX, to very futuristic modern reinterpretations. In the end the final design was somewhere in the middle of the two, with elements from both.

Even the air box is part of the frame, with the engine taking the strain as a stressed member. In what is believed to be another first, the Concept KX also has a single-sided softail rear end. As gorgeous as it is, Enfield insists that this bike is purely a concept and is not destined for production.

The truth is, in the company's home market, it just would not be a viable offering and could only be built profitably if Royal Enfield could be sure of selling it in more affluent countries, especially the USA. So the future of the KX Concept will depend how the INT 650 and the Continental GT 650 sell there, although pitching Royal Enfield's US headquarters and flagship dealership at 226

North Water Street in Milwaukee is a tanks on the lawn move. After all, Milwaukee is a place name most associated with that famous vendor of V-twins, Harley-Davidson. Ironically, just as Royal Enfield's engine sizes grow in the USA, Harley-Davidson – the US market leader in heavyweight motorcycles by a large margin – plans to introduce smaller, sub-500cc motorcycles into international markets such as India. As selling motorcycles gets harder, so do the tactics.

Lal doesn't seem fazed and is clear that his company has ambitions to lead and expand the middleweight motorcycle segment worldwide. At the US launch of the new twins he announced that: 'In international markets the twins will play a strategic role not just for us but for the industry to expand the mid-weight segment and invite new users into the category.' Rudratej Singh, president of Royal Enfield, followed up with a press release declaring that the company 'expect the Interceptor INT 650 and the Continental GT 650 to represent the perfect opportunity to upgrade commuters in South East Asia and Latin America, as well as expand the motorcycling segment in USA and Europe'. If the latter proves to be the case, expect Royal Enfield to build a competitor to Harley-Davidson's V-twins and start chasing

An Interceptor in an Indian sunset. ROYAL ENFIELD

affluent European and American buyers. After all, the company has a fine history of building V-twins and a heritage that most manufacturers can only dream of.

The rumour mill insists that the KX, or something very like it, will go into production. Fundamentals being disclosed, such as the 80mm bore and 83.8mm stroke and a power output 'close to 100hp through a six-speed transmission', are irrelevant if it's just a display mule. There are many people in the motorcycle business who feel they're just hanging on to their jobs until the industry is wiped out by electric scooters for those who need transport, and experiences such as exotic holidays or skydiving for the thrill seekers. But nobody told Royal Enfield as it heads towards an annual production that should soon exceed a million motorcycles. Just as the company survived the mass extinction of the British motorcycle industry, it looks like it might be a saviour of motorcycling. The future's bright – the future's an Orange Crush Royal Enfield Interceptor.

The future's bright – the future's an Orange Crush Interceptor.

The staircase to the clubhouse – keep riding indeed.

INDEX

RELATED TITLES FROM CROWOOD

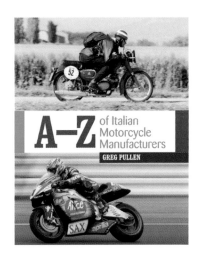

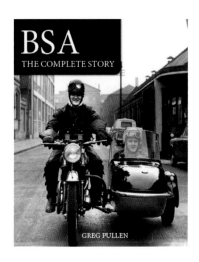

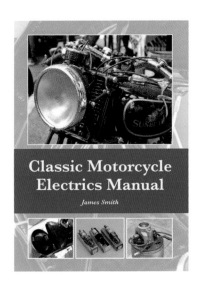

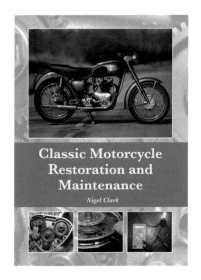

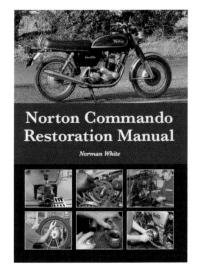

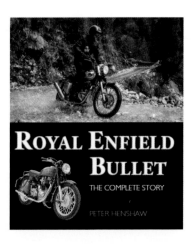